HOW TO GET GOVERNMENT GRANTS

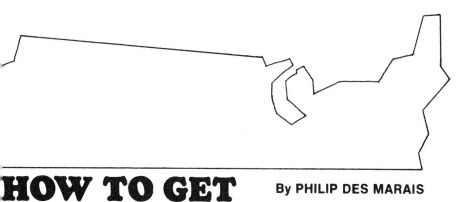

HOW TO GET
GOVERNMENT GRANTS

By PHILIP DES MARAIS

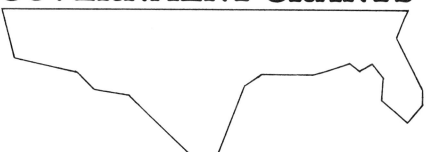

Public
Service
Materials
Center

Contents

336.012

D463

Introduction

In the profession of fund raising for education, health, cultural, and social service programs — securing government grants has been described as the grandest frontier of them all.

The "Catalog of Federal Domestic Assistance" includes 975 programs administered by 52 different Federal departments, independent agencies, and other organizations. The gamut of government grants is literally from "Academic Computing Services" to "Zoo Display Animals."

Confronted with this vast array of grant possibilities in the Federal government, as well as programs from the State and local level, the college president, hospital administrator, public official, or agency head naturally wonders how and where do we start to qualify for and receive or increase grant support for our institution.

How to Get Government Grants has three main purposes: First, it describes how an eligible institution gets organized to qualify for government funding. This may require action by the Board of Trustees and development of new or augmented administrative and staff functions in the organization.

Secondly, it presents a system and a process by which an institution identifies the programs and sources of government funds for which it is eligible to apply.

And, thirdly, it provides a plan for developing proposals and applications for grants and contracts; the basics of a management system for grants received; and, in conclusion, a checklist of primary information sources for government funding.

How to Get Government Grants is not a manual on proposal writing or on how to fill out an application for a grant. That is something you learn by doing. Neither is it intended to be a catalog or listing of government grant programs, but it tells you where to get them.

The information presented in this publication is based on 14 years of experience by the author in the field of government programs. For 8 years, I served as a Deputy Assistant Secretary of the U.S. Department of Health, Education and Welfare, primarily involved in legislative planning and development for Federal aid programs. At Fordham University, I have had the opportunity to establish a system of sponsored research, education, and service programs, funded in large part from government grants.

I owe a great debt to numerous colleagues at H.E.W., dedicated civil servants with high professional qualifications, with whom I was associated in planning for the grant programs of that gigantic department. At Fordham, knowledgeable and determined faculty and staff have worked with me to demonstrate that the opportunities and possibilities of government support can be brought to reality, to strengthen and augment the research and teaching capabilities of a large urban university.

I salute the expertise of the Office of Research Services staff. Edward Leight, III designs grant budgets and writes financial reports. Thomas De Julio reviews all project grant expenditures with a legal eye. Rita Smith, administrative secretary, is in charge of grant files and records, and information systems. All of these colleagues have contributed to what knowledge this book provides, on the challenging and rewarding process of getting government grants.

PHILIP DES MARAIS

CHAPTER 1

Process and Policy ....
For Government Grants.

The process for securing government grants requires a total involvement of the institution, from the governing board and the top administrators, to the most junior professional staff members whose work would be supported by grant funds.

Institutional Grants Policy

The decision to seek government funds for support of schools and colleges, hospitals and health services, and other community service programs is inevitable and unavoidable.

There are at least two compelling factors to be considered; the magnitude and scope of government funds available, and the fact that the constituency will expect that your institution is qualifying for available government funds.

In the area of higher education alone, for example, total

Federal obligations (grants and contracts) to colleges and universities amounted to 3 billion 480 million dollars, in fiscal year 1971 (1971-72). By fiscal year 1974, the funding level of the U.S. Office of Education reached 5.9 billion dollars. OE administers programs covering virtually every level and aspect of education. This is exclusive of aid to health programs and hospitals, and social service programs, which account for at least another 4 billion dollars. Contrast these amounts with the slightly less than 2.4 billion dollars of total grants from all private foundations, for all purposes, in those same years.

There is an almost universal expectation these days of the availability of Federal funds. I suggest that those in charge of our institutions, board of directors and chief administrators, have a moral and professional obligation to assure that the institution, its program, staff, and clientele benefit from all government funds available.

Legislative History

During the decades of the 1950 and 60's, important policy decisions were made in this country, by the voters and taxpayers, through their representatives in Congress. Basic social legislation was enacted or expanded: The National Science Foundation Act; the National Defense Education Act; the Social Security Amendments of 1963; the Vocational Rehabilitation Act; the Higher Education Facilities Act of 1963; the Elementary and Secondary Education Act of 1965; the Higher Education Act of 1965; the Medical Care Amendments to the Social Security Act; up through the Education Amendments of 1972.

By means of this and related legislation, the American people decided that their tax funds would become an integral part of the funding of health, education, and welfare programs serving all citizens of the country. Thus, we now have three categories of financial support:

A. The traditional subsidies from charitable and religious endowments, grants, and foundations;

B. Fees charged for services; and

C. Federal as well as state and local governmental grants and allotments.

The government grant funds flow to the institution, their programs, and clientele through a bewildering and complex variety of formulas, allotments, and channels.

Institutional Commitments

Once the governing board of the institution has made the policy decision to seek or expand government funding, the assignment of responsibility is made to the operating head, who is ultimately the chief grants officer.

In making this decision, several important assumptions are implicit.

1. As a private agency, it is willing to undertake the responsibility of public accountability for all funds and disclosures to government granting agencies of information about the fiscal and professional aspects of its program.

2. As a public or private institution (school, hospital, university, etc.), it is willing and able to meet requirements of

Federal regulations and guidelines, i.e., to maintain policies of non-discrimination, equal opportunity, and affirmative action for equal employment policies. (These same regulations apply to programs receiving state and local funds.) In addition, there are the fiscal management requirements, subject to a post-audit by government auditors.

3. The programs of the institutions, and the professional staff operating them will be of the character, quality, and scope necessary to qualify for grant support. Government grants are available invariably only to those institutions which meet certain professional and legal qualifications. They must have acceditation by educational and professional associations. For example, colleges and universities, by the regional accrediting associations; hospitals, by the Joint Accrediting Commission; schools, under the jurisdiction of "local public education agencies"; social service programs, "licensed by the State Department of Welfare." Such requirements are specifically provided for in legislation authorizing grant programs.

4. The chief executive officer will provide administrative support and leadership to the securing of grants and contracts. This means staff support, support services, and budgetary authority for grant administrators.

Institutional Responsibility

Institutional review, approval, and administration of all sponsored grant programs should be centered in one staff position or office. This unit should have both vertical and horizontal access to all elements of the institution.

If there is no such staff position in the institution, a designation is needed so that responsibility and coordination can be fixed and controlled.

This office must be in a position to deal with all administrative, professional, and financial elements of the institution.

The government grant process involves all parts of the institution.

a) The top administration, which must officially "authorize" the proposal or application for a grant.

b) The professional staff, which must plan the program for which financial support is being sought and which will actually carry out the program, if the grant is awarded.

c) The financial office, which must be custodian of the funds, makes disbursements under proper authorization and prepares interim and final financial reports of grant expenditures.

Getting the Grant Process Moving

Administrative and staff responsibility for the grant programs has to be clearly established in a designated office. These operations have various names, such as Vice President for Research and Sponsored Programs, Office of Sponsored Programs, Director of Sponsored Programs, or Office of Research Services.

But whatever the name, three essential functions are centered there:

1. This office takes the initiative in assisting the professional staff in identifying programs and sources of funds for research and training projects.

2. The head of the office is the authorized official for signing proposals for submission to granting agencies.

3. The director supervises the establishment of the program budget after the grant is received and participates in the fiscal management of the project. Such an operation uniquely combines administrative, professional, and fiscal activities.

When an institution is able to combine grant information, application review and approval, and grant administration in one office, it has achieved its first objective — organization — for a successful grant process.

Administrative and Professional Staff Roles

As indicated earlier, the sponsored program office works with administrative and professional staff in identifying possible grant programs and preparation of proposals, essentially a supportive service. Some administrator, or professional staff member, must take responsibility as project director for each government grant, as required by regulations.

Developing Information Systems

The need for current and comprehensive information about government grant programs is a vital element of grant operations.

There is the need for an *internal system* which informs the staff about institutional procedures for development and approval of grant applications. This procedure probably should be documented in an official memorandum on policies and guidelines for sponsored programs. If such a policy statement is feasible for adoption by the governing board and for incorporation into institutional by-laws, it then becomes, in fact, a part of any grant award or contract. These guidelines should be distributed periodically, to all personnel who would be involved in grant activities.

Providing a regular and systematic flow of grant program information to the staff is essential. Government granting agencies regularly mail program guides and application information to all agencies eligible to apply for grants. These mailings are usually addressed to the head of the institution.

Grant Information Center

Once established, the Sponsored Programs Office becomes the center for all information about government grant programs.

Any other administrative office in the institution that receives grant publications should immediately forward them to the Sponsored Program Director.

Major sources of grant information that can be utilized are as follows:

1. Program guides and announcements from Federal agencies. (An annotated listing of major Federal program guides is provided in Chapter VIII.)

2. The Congressional Record: You get this free by asking your Representative in the U.S. Congress, from the Congressional District in which your institution is located, to put you on his mailing list. By keeping up with the "Record" with its daily reports on the debates of the U.S. Congress, you gradually develop a sense of what's coming down the pipeline by way of government grant programs and, most important, the funds appropriated for them.

3. The Federal Register: This official publication is used by Executive Departments of the Federal Government to announce all guidelines and regulations for grant programs. Announcements of *contract* solicitation for research and train-

ing activities are included in the Federal Register. These notices give a brief description of the needs of the Federal programs, and an address or phone number to be used to secure a "Request for A Proposal". RFP's, as they are known, are sent to eligible institutions on a discretionary basis, only after the institution has expressed its own special interest in being given an opportunity to submit a proposal.

4. Publications from Professional Associations: Every institution eligible for government grants usually belongs to one or more national professional associations. Examples include the American Council on Education, the American Hospital Association, the Association of American Colleges, the American Association of Junior Colleges, etc.

All of these groups publish bulletins, usually from their Washington offices, containing current information about grant programs for their member institutions.

5. Newspapers and Magazines: The Washington Post carries more detailed reporting on Federal aid and government grant programs than any other daily source. By following program developments —

- legislation introduced in the Congress

- bills being reviewed in Congressional Committee hearings

- legislation passed by Congress, and

- appropriations being provided,

the Director for Sponsored Programs develops valuable "lead time" on Federal programs. He is able to identify, months in advance, possible new grant sources. Faculty and staff can be

advised of these developments, and program planning, leading
to possible applications and proposals, can get under way.

Program Reports and Newsletters

When a Sponsored Program Office is serving more than 25
staff persons who are potential applicants for specific grant
programs, an in-house information bulletin on current grant
sources is a valuable information tool.

Many institutions also use such a bulletin to announce
grants received, as well as opportunities for grant programs
particularly suited to the interests and capabilities of the institution and its professional staff or the clientele being served
by its programs.

Controlling the Flood

When the grant information system is in full operation, every
day's mail brings program information to the Office for Sponsored Programs. It then becomes the task of the Office to sift
through the flood of publications and bulletins and identify
those that apply to the institution.

Relevant information can be included in the bulletins going
to staff, and special referrals can be made, if deadlines for
proposals are limited.

Experienced grants office administrators invariably report
that the widest possible dissemination of information within
the institution is the best policy. The more people in your
agency who know about grant funds available, proposals
being submitted, and grants received, the better. The spirit of
professional pride, intra-institutional competition, and collaborative efforts are essential elements of an expanding program of grants for sponsored research, training and services.

Fiscal Management Systems

There are three key elements in the fiscal management system for government grants:

1. The official signing of proposals and applications for grants on behalf of the institution.

2. A special accounting system which establishes a restricted account budget for each grant, with assigned authority to expend the funds, and

3. A procedure for recording expenditures from grant budgets, so that periodic statements of expenditure are produced and are available for necessary interim and final financial reports to be sent to the granting agencies as required.

The special requirements of the Federal government and more detailed aspects of grants management will be dealt with in Chapter V. But, there are some necessary decisions which can be made in advance and will save a lot of trouble in the future, providing incentives and support for the government grant programs.

Institutional Approval

Effective delegation of authority to sign proposals on behalf of the institution is often one of the most crucial decisions in establishing a government grants system. The effort should be to keep the signing process as simple and as swift as possible.

One of the purposes of having an Office for Sponsored Programs is to give proposal signing authority to that office. Any necessary internal review of proposals should be clarified in institutional procedures. But the important factor to be stressed is that staff know that one office can take care of all their clearance and signing procedures.

Spending Grant Funds

Once a grant award has been received, a system should be in place to provide for

1. Establishing an operating budget;

2. Authorizing and reviewing expenditures, and

3. Actual disbursement of funds.

Again, it is vital for the Sponsored Programs Office to be in the center of these operations. The function to be stressed here is to have a responsible unit in the institution with the primary concern that grant expenditures are made according to the terms and conditions of the granting agency, while respecting the professional responsibility of the staff in charge of the program.

The division of labor can be neatly allocated by providing for the project director to authorize expenditures, the Sponsored Programs Office to have a review function, and the finance office to make the actual disbursement, according to regular institutional policies on disbursement of funds.

Expenditure Reports

All government grants are given for a specific period of time, usually called, "the budget period", normally 12 months. At a minimum, a financial report is required within 60 days of the end of the budget period.

The report is submitted on a form that calls for a display of figures showing the amount spent for each category of the budget, i.e., personnel salaries, secretarial services, supplies, equipment, travel, etc.

From time to time, auditors from the Federal government

visit your institution. They examine records about the program operation and expenditure of funds from grants. If grant funds are revealed to have been spent for unauthorized purposes, an audit exception is reported, and the institution is liable to be billed for unauthorized expenditures.

Hence, the requirement for an accurate expenditure reporting system. It can also serve an important program need by providing the project director with regular reports on the status of the grant budget.

In summary, before any application for government funds is submitted, your institution should have agreed on a plan that assigns authority to approve and authorize grant proposals, determines the method for establishing grant budgets and spending the funds, and provides for an accurate monthly and annual report of expenditures for each grant award.

Program Survey for Government Grants

"Why can't we get a government grant for our program"? is a question often asked of administrators by their board members or staff.

On numerous occasions, I have been called upon by executives of education, health or social service agencies to meet with members of the staff and the trustees or directors to discuss "how we can qualify for more government funds." There is, invariably, a situation of a very generalized awareness of government grants. There is a concern that their institution is not getting its fair share of tax support. There is an urgent demand that something be done about this.

My advice to the board and the harried administrators is that they first do a careful survey of possible government grant programs.

Grant funds become a reality when a dynamic equation is operating as follows:

The objectives, programs, professional manpower resources, and facilities of the institution are equal to the requirements, qualifications and purposes of a specific grant program. "You have to be eligible"!

Making the critical determination is really a parallel process:

a) Discovering more precisely just what government grant programs your institution can qualify for,

b) Discussion and dialogue with your own staff about available grant programs, and their potential and interest for the staff and programs of the institution.

When I opened the Office of Research Services at Fordham University, I spent the first six weeks visiting with faculty and staff including seven graduate and professional deans and twenty-seven department chairmen. I wanted to find out about what grants they had been getting. Were there specific grant programs they wanted more information about? What were the special interests and concerns of their faculties and departments? What personal contacts and experience with granting agencies were already in existence? Could these be expanded? Had grant support been of genuine benefit to the department's program? What problems had been encountered in the management of grant received? What kind of additional services and assistance did they need in order to prepare more proposals or to seek wider grant support?

These initial conferences with the staff provided an opportunity to suggest new channels and possibilities for grant support. An inventory of information requests about grant programs was being developed.

The challenge to the Office of Sponsored Programs is twofold: to develop a comprehensive knowledge of available grant programs applicable to the institution; and a sensitive and keen assessment of the interests and capabilities of the staff, which can be matched with the grant opportunities.

Finally, trustees, administrators, and professional staff must become aware of a central element of the grant process.

Research, training, and other proposals submitted to government agencies for support undergo a review by panels of peers and other experts — often in a national competition. Your resources have to measure up to standards of excellence. The award of a government grant is, indeed, a recognition of the merit and professional competence of your program, as well as providing welcome financial support.

CHAPTER 2

Grant Agencies and Programs

The Washington Connection

Despite all of the proposals for Federal revenue sharing with the states and planning for decentralization of Federal programs, Washington, D.C. is still the hub of government grant activity.

The basic decisions to establish Federal government grant programs is made by Congressional legislation. The annual appropriation of funds for grant programs takes place in Washington. The administration of all grant programs, including those channeled through state and local government agencies, is centered in Washington.

The initial impulse of an administrator or staff member assigned to work on government grants is to want to take a trip to Washington. However, understanding and useful knowledge of the Washington grant scene can be developed at the home base. After this process is under way, visits to granting agencies in Washington can be productive and even necessary.

There are at least three vital sources of information and channels to granting agencies which should be explored in the grant planning process:

1) The Office of the U.S. Representative for the Congressional district in which your institution is located.

2) Staff of your institution who were previously employed by agencies of the Federal government.

3) The information systems and the publications available from the granting agencies themselves.

The Congressional Office

Any organization eligible for grant support should, as a matter of regular policy, be in touch with its representative in Congress. He needs to know about your program, how it serves his constituents, and to what extent the agency participates in grant programs for which he has responsibility as a legislator.

As your agency gets organized for a new or renewed push for grant support, a formal request should be made for a meeting with the Congressman and members of his staff. The administrator in charge of grant development and the chief executive officer or Board chairman should represent the institution. It should be understood at the outset that you are looking for information, assistance, and support, but *not influence*. 90% of all Federal grants are made without special intercession by members of Congress or partisan political pull.

If your Representative is a member of a committee that handles legislation for program areas similar to your institution's (i.e., education, public health, public welfare, sciences, etc.), he should have a specialized knowledge of programs. If he happens to be a member of an appropriation sub-committee (i.e., sub-committee on Labor and H.E.W. of the Committee on Appropriations) that votes on allocation for grant programs in your area, his ability to be of help can be crucial and decisive. It is no coincidence that since Senator Warren Magnuson of Washington has been Chairman of the Senate Appropriations Sub-committee for Health, Education, and Welfare that the University of Washington at Seattle has moved up to #3 in the nation in Federal grants awarded, totaling $67 million in 1973!

After the Congressman has been given a factual briefing on your program and grant needs (this could include a visit by him to your campus, hospital, research center), you ask him for some concrete assistance. Get on his mailing list for the Congressional Record. Have his office do some initial research on Federal programs applicable to your institution. Request help in getting program information and publications from the granting agencies. Subsequently, you may request his assistance in getting initial appointments with granting agencies in Washington.

Finally, ask to have a staff person designated as your contact with the office. Many Congressmen have experienced staff who are known as "case workers." They have developed expertise in communicating with Federal agencies on behalf of constituents. If you're lucky, your Congressman can be of real assistance. If this does not prove to be the case, you should find this out for yourself.

The Former Federal Executive

One of the most effective shortcuts to Federal program information and grant support is to employ a former Federal government executive.

An examination of the list of 100 colleges and universities receiving the largest amounts of Federal funds in 1973 is interesting in connection with top former Federal officials now associated with these institutions.

Massachusetts Institute of Technology heads the list with $125 million. The President of M.I.T. is the former White House Science Advisor to the President of the United States. The Director of Government Relations at Harvard was a former staff assistant to President Kennedy. The President of the University of Minnesota was a former presidential assistant. A former Secretary of Health, Education, and Welfare is a key dean at the University of Michigan. The Vice President for Medical Affairs at Penn is a former Surgeon General of the U.S. Another former Surgeon General is Dean of the L.S.U. Medical School. A former staff member of the President's Science Advisory Committee is Director of Government Relations at Cornell. The former Director of the National Institutes of Health is advisor to the President, Rockefeller University. The former Assistant Secretary for Administration of H.E.W. has been Vice President of Georgetown University and then Vice Chancellor of the giant State University of New York System.

In providing these examples, I am not suggesting that there has been any conflict of interest involved. The fact that a former Federal government official is now a university dean will not gain for his institution special favor or consideration for grant applications. The benefit derives from the intimate personal knowledge of government programs that such a person possesses. The scope of knowledge of government programs also varies with experience. A former member of the Science

Advisory Committee or top official of the Bureau of the Budget will have a government-wide perspective. A former Public Health Service officer will be knowledgeable about P.H.S. programs; likewise, for an ex-U.S. Office of Education staff member.

In the National Science Foundation, there is a continual movement back and forth between campus science departments and NSF staff units. A specific case is that of a Fordham physics professor who was an NSF physics area program director for two years. The unit administered review of research grant proposals on a nationwide basis. The scientist then accepted an offer of the chairmanship of the Department of Physics at an expanding State University. From the university's point of view, his experience as a program director in the National Science Foundation is a valuable asset in guiding faculty to the research grant route.

In connection with the National Science Foundation, I had a recent discussion with a member of the House of Representatives who is a senior member of the appropriations subcommittee responsible for NSF appropriations. His Congressional district happens to include one of the nation's leading universities. He reported that he receives a great deal of helpful information and opinions about programs of the NSF from the faculty of the university. This dialogue is illustrative of the kind of communication that provides a basis for successful grant support.

Government Agency Publications and Reports

All Federal agencies are required by law to provide information about grant programs to all citizens requesting such information. But with nearly 1,000 specific grant programs in operation, the problem for a possible grantee is to know what to ask for.

Some programs such as the operating agencies of the Department of Health, Education and Welfare have a policy of sending program announcements and booklets to heads of eligible grantees. University and college presidents receive notification of all grant programs in higher education administered by the Office of Education. The National Science Foundation has the most comprehensive series of program booklets and bulletins. A written request will get an organization on the mailing list.

It has been suggested that the Congressional Office be asked to assist in getting your organization on the mailing list of government agencies with grant programs relevant to its program needs. Finally, the importance of establishing a central location in the institution for program information cannot be overstressed. The information needs to be kept up to date, analyzed for local applications, and be accessible to all staff who can participate in developing grant proposals. As mentioned, Chapter VIII of this book contains an annotated checklist of program publications and information sources which should be assembled in order to have necessary program information currently available.

Identifying Grant Programs and Agencies

In developing an overall picture of grant possibilities, it is useful to have special targets and objectives to guide your search.

1. What and where are the major granting agencies?

2. Which are the largest grant programs in the agencies? It is important to identify those programs which have sufficient funds to make an application worthwhile.

3. Which are the agencies and programs most relevant to your institution?

4. Are there current changes in funding levels and program priorities which would influence your grant application plans? It is very frustrating, for example, to have staff working up a proposal for a grant only to be advised that Congress has cut the appropriation for the program and new applications are being rejected.

Major Federal Granting Agencies

To make any sense out of the vast array of government grant programs, it is helpful to develop a concept of the "geography" of government agencies and programs.

It is not intended in this survey to present a detailed or comprehensive analysis of agencies and their programs. This can best be achieved by a careful study of agency publications themselves. The following outline is designed to illustrate program and grant relationships between Federal agencies and grantee organizations in the education, health service, social and community service, cultural and scientific research fields:

Granting Agencies	Grantees

I. U.S. DEPARTMENT OF
HEALTH, EDUCATION, &
WELFARE

    A. U.S. Office of Education

        Local Education Agencies
        State Departments of Education
        Vocational Education Agencies
        Institutions of Higher Education
          Grants & loans to students
          Teacher Training
          International Education
          Graduate Fellowships
          Community Colleges
          Developing Institutions
        Proprietary and Independent Post-secondary schools

    B. U.S. Public Health Service

        Hospital Construction
        Migrant Health Services
        State Department of Health

    1) National Institutes of Health

        Medical Schools
        University Graduate Faculties
          Biomedical
          Chemical
          Psychology
          Social Service
          Sociology

    2) National Institute of
       Alcoholism and Drug Abuse

        State Drug Abuse Agencies
        Local Addiction Agencies
        University Science Faculties
          Medical Schools
        Institutions of Higher Education
        Community Service Agencies

    C. Rehabilitation Services
       Administration

        State Welfare Departments
        Child Welfare Agencies
        Family Planning Agencies
        Legal Services Agencies

D. Social & Rehabilitation Services	State Agencies for the Handicapped Mental Retardation Agencies, Programs for Cerebral Palsy Epilepsy Vocational Rehabilitation Agencies for Mentally and Physically handicapped, blind, deaf.
E. Administration on Aging	State Agencies for Aging Senior Citizens Programs
II. NATIONAL SCIENCE FOUNDATION	College and University Faculty in Mathematical Physical Medical Biological Social, and Enginering Sciences Institutions of Higher Education Departments of Science Graduate Fellowships Academic, Nonprofit, and Commercial Sciences Research Institutes
III. NATIONAL ENDOWMENT FOR THE ARTS	State Arts Councils Opera Companies Symphony Orchestras Museums Professional Theatre Dance Companies Artists-in-Residence at educational institutions Painters, sculptors, printmakers, photographers Commissions for Public Works of Art

Granting Agencies	Grantees
IV. NATIONAL ENDOWMENT FOR THE HUMANITIES	Institutions of Higher Education Education Programs and Research Projects in Modern and Classical Languages Literature, History, Jurisprudence, Philosophy, Archeology, Comparative Religion, Ethics, Humanities aspects of social sciences.
V. U.S. DEPARTMENT OF JUSTICE Law Enforcement Assistance Administration.	State Crime Control Commission Local Criminal Justice Councils Police Departments States Attorneys Offices State Police Departments Institutions of Higher Education Law Enforcement Education Programs Law Enforcement and Criminal Justice Research Juvenile Delinquency Control and Prevention Agencies
VI. U.S. DEPARTMENT OF DEFENSE A. Air Force, Office of Scientific Research	Non-profit Scientific Research Organizations Institutions of Higher Education Research Projects in Chemistry, Mathematical, Informational, Electronic, Solid State, Life Sciences, General Physics, etc.
B. U.S. Army Research Office	Institutions of Higher Education Non-profit Research Institutes Projects in Geosciences, Life Sciences, Electronics, Metallurgy, Chemistry, Physics, Mathematics

C. Office of Naval Research	Institutions of Higher Education
	Research Institutes
	Projects in all areas of basic scientific research
VII. U.S. DEPARTMENT OF LABOR	State Departments of Vocational Education
Manpower Administration	Vocational Schools and Institutions
	Institutions of Higher Education

State Government

Most state agencies and departments operate with mandated allotments of Federal funds—to be used for grants to state and local, public and private agencies in health, education and social services.

The Catalogue of Federal Domestic Assistance provides information which identifies the state agency making grants of Federal funds for programs on the local level, both public and private.

Local Government Agencies with Federal Grant Funds

1. *Local Education Agencies:*

Local public school systems are the grantee recipients for all funds allocated under the Elementary and Secondary Education Act of 1965 as amended. Grants are available to provide special education services for disadvantaged children, textbooks, and supplementary education services for all elementary and secondary school children in the district, enrolled in both public and private schools. Proposals for grants under this major Federal aid program must be channeled through the local education agency to the State Department of Education.

2. Local Public Welfare Departments

Federal funds for child welfare services, day care programs, family planning services, special services to the elderly, and handicapped, are channeled through the Welfare departments in counties, towns, and cities. Grant applications to support these services, to be provided by either public or private agencies, must be submitted initially on the local level.

Often there is a lack of information or resistance from the local public agency as to the eligibility of private agencies for these grants. In these cases, the assistance and information provided by the district's U.S. Representative can be most effective. It is in his interest to assure that all of his constituents eligible for Federal grants are aided. His office can serve as a mediator among local agencies applying for equitable shares of Federal grant programs.

Getting Into the National Scene

Given the fact that availability of government grants is the result of national policy decisions, national organizations have an important role in the grant process. Such groups are the National Education Association, American Medical Association, American Council on Education, National AFL-CIO, American Hospital Association, National Catholic Education Association, National Council of Catholic Charities — and many others — are busily involved in testifying before Congressional committees in favor of Federal aid for their particular programs. All of these organizations have Washington offices with staffs that monitor Federal grant and aid programs.

Operating programs and agencies seeking grant support will naturally look to their national professional organization for assistance and information. Most national organizations provide periodic bulletins to members, with information on Federal legislation related to grants and on the availability of grant programs in their areas of interest.

Leaders of professional associations who are also directors of operating agencies are asked to testify before legislative committees on the need for and effectiveness of grant programs.

Experienced administrators and professionals who become involved in this activity necessarily develop a sophisticated understanding of the whole grant process from Congressional committee hearings to the receiving of an actual grant award announcement which authorizes the funds to support the program of the institution.

CHAPTER 3

Grants, Contracts, and Entitlements*

Federal, state, and local governments make funds available to educational, health, and social service institutions and programs by means of a variety of granting and allotment procedures. Qualifying for these funds requires an accurate knowledge of the various funding mechanisms.

Entitlement and Formula Grants

Some of the major government grant programs provide funds on the basis of entitlements, and the funds are distributed according to an allotment formula provided for in the law.

Entitlement refers to a particular kind of institution or program being eligible for a grant by the very fact of its existence and functions.

*Material in this chapter is based on H.E.W. Grants Administration Manual, Part I, General, Contract or Grant 5/17/74.

Formula grants provide that the amount of the grant is based on some economic or operational factor which is used to measure the eligibility for funding. These two concepts can best be illustrated with the following typical examples:

1. *Veterans Cost-of-Instruction Program:*
   Institutions of Higher Education are entitled to grants under this program provided they enroll certain minimum numbers of veterans receiving veterans' benefits under the G.I. Bill; the institution must maintain at least one full-time professional counselor serving veteran students, and must increase its veteran student enrollment by 10% over the previous year to be eligible for a grant. The formula for the grant is x number of dollars per veteran enrolled depending upon the size of the Federal appropriation for the program.

2. *Elementary & Secondary Education Act of 1965, Title II Grants for Instructional Materials:*
   All elementary and secondary schools are eligible for an allotment for textbooks and other institutional materials based on their enrollment figures in a given school year. The formula for the grant has been averaging about $15 per pupil per year.

3. *Health Manpower Act:*
   Institutional Support for Medical, Dental, and related health professions:
   1) Capitation grants
   2) Educational initiatives
   3) Other institutional support
   Under this program, which had an appropriation of $320 million in 1974, every accredited medical, dental, and veterinary medicine school is *entitled* to a grant based upon these components of a formula. The capita-

tion grant provides an award based simply on the number of students enrolled.

4. *Public Law 480, Overseas Relief Grants:*
The Agency for International Development of the U.S. Department of State provides grants for emergency and disaster assistance, and social development projects — to people in need, in foreign countries.

Voluntary, religious, social welfare, and relief organizations registered with the Office of Private and Voluntary Cooperation of A.I.D. are *entitled* to grants and other forms of financial assistance for their projects — if they meet the criteria as provided in the law. As of December 31, there were 91 organizations voluntarily registered with the Agency for International Development's Committee on Voluntary Foreign Aid. During the 1973 reporting period, these agencies received government support in the form of grants, contracts, excess property, P.L. 480 donated food, and transportation costs for overseas freight, totaling $208 million.

5. *New York State Aid to Private Colleges and Universities (Bundy Act):*
All accredited private institutions of higher education in New York State (not under sectarian control) receive an annual grant based on the number of degrees awarded in a given twelve-month period, i.e., $800 per B.A. degree, $600 per M.A. and J.D. degrees, and $3,000 per Ph.D. degree.

Project Grants

When consideration is given to seeking government financial assistance, people are usually thinking about project grants.
Grants are the appropriate instrument for government aid

when authorizing or appropriations legislation mandates their use. They are awarded to eligible grantees when the following purposes are intended:

1. The program objective is general financial assistance to state or local units of government or non-profit organizations or individuals eligible under specific legislation authorizing such assistance.

2. Financial assistance to support a *specific program activity* of state and local government, non-profit organizations or individuals under specific legislation authorizing such assistance.

3. When funds are available to provide financial assistance to programs or projects requiring creative and professional efforts such as basic research in the sciences and humanities, innovative program planning for education or professional training, and for areas of activity for which competitive proposals are desired. The effort in this type of program-project grant is to "support excellence." The award process usually involves an objective review and rating of proposals by panels of professional peers from outside the granting agency.

4. The project grant method is also used as a protection against government control over the details of curriculum, program design or performance.

The National Institutes of Health have pioneered in the development of sophisticated project grant review systems. National panels of scholars and scientists are regularly appointed to review research and training grant proposals. The review process for major grants (over $100,000), will often include a "site visit." Members of the review panel will visit the institution submitting the proposal, talk with the professional staff and evaluate "on the spot" the resources and capabilities of the proposed grantee.

Different Project Grant Functions — i.e., Research, Training, Technical Assistance, Service, and Facilities and Equipment:

In planning for development of a government grant proposal, it is necessary to decide exactly what kind of a grant is being sought.

The 1975 Congressional appropriation for the *National Science Foundation* is a good illustration of the variety of project grants available from just this one agency of the Federal government.

NSF APPROPRIATION — FY 1975

		Budget Request	Autho- rization Bill	Appro- priation Bill
		(in millions of dollars)		
1)	Scientific Research Project Support . . .	$363.7	$358.7	not specified
2)	National and Special Research Programs	84.8	91.9	not specified
3)	National Research Centers	52.5	52.5	not specified
4)	Science Information Activities	5.0	6.3	$ 5.0
5)	International Cooperative Scientific Activities	8.0	8.0	not specified
6)	Research Applied to National Needs . .	148.9	148.9	143.4
7)	Intergovernmental Science and Research Utilization	1.0	2.0	1.0
8)	Institutional Improvement for Science .	3.0	12.0	5.5
9)	Graduate Student Support	12.7	15.0	13.2
10)	Science Education Improvement	61.4	70.0	65.15
11)	Planning and Policy Studies	2.7	2.7	2.7
12)	Program Development and Management	39.5	39.5	38.1
	Sub-Total	$783.2	$807.5	$763.3*
	Special Foreign Currency	5.0	5.0	4.85
	TOTAL	**$788.2**	**$812.5**	**$768.15**

*Total includes 101.8 million passed as part of the special energy appropriation and $661.5 million passed as part of the regular NSF appropriation.

NSF organizes its grants under twelve program-project areas. However, most grant programs come under the following categories:

1. *Research:* project grants are made for a specific basic research study to be conducted by one or more professional staff members of the grantee institution. This is the largest single category of grants at NSF, as indicated in the preceding table, with $358.7 million authorized for research grants.

2. *Training:* training grants are made for the purpose of supporting some kind of academic instructional project such as in-service training of teachers or other professional personnel or professional training of graduate and professional students. In the NSF program, these kinds of grants are covered under items 9 and 10.

3. *Technical Assistance:* technical assistance grants provide funds for staff and consultants on the project to give professional assistance and consultation to other institutions or community agencies in need of such assistance.

4. *Service:* grants for special service projects simply provide funds to enable the grantee to provide or expand the services which the institution normally provides in its own program.

5. *Facilities and Equipment:* major Federal grant programs have involved projects exclusively for facilities (buildings, laboratories, hospitals, schools, university libraries), and the equipment for such facilities.

Contracts: for Research, Training, Technical Assistance, Service

"What is the difference between a Federal *grant* and a *con-*

tract?" is a logical question often asked. The answer lies in understanding the purpose of the Federal aid provided.

If the purpose of the aid program is primarily to provide funds to assist units of state or local government, or private institutions, or individuals to achieve their own program objective and goals, the form of aid is usually that of a *grant.*

When funds are awarded by a Federal or other government agency to another agency, public or private, using the contract method of award, the Federal agency is involved essentially in purchasing assistance or services in carrying out its own statutorily assigned mission of service to the people.

Specific Uses of Contracts

1. Contracts are used for all procurements — for the acquisition of goods and services, or property (facilities) by government agencies, for their own programs and activities.

2. Several types of procurement utilize the contract procedure.

A) *Evaluation,* which means assessment of the performance of government programs (including grant programs) or any type of grantee activity desired or required by the granting agency. (Congress often requires evaluation reports on the progress of grant programs or the use of grant funds.) Every grant to schools under the Elementary and Secondary Education Act of 1965 carried an allotment of funds to pay for an evaluation study which the school was required to contract for.

B) *Technical Assistance,* which includes professional or technical support services provided to the government as a third party.

C) *Surveys and Study,* which provide specific information desired by a government agency.

D) *Consulting* or personal services of all kinds (usually of professional character), whether conducted for a government agency or for a third party.

E) *Training projects,* where the government agency selects the individuals or specific groups whose members are to be trained, or specifies the content or curriculum of the program.

F) *Planning services* for agency use.

G) *Production* of publications or audio-visual materials.

H) *Design* or development of items for agency use.

I) *Conferences* conducted for a government agency.

To summarize the objectives of the grant vs. the contract procedure, it could be argued that if an organization desires to provide assistance or services to the government, a contract is proposed. If an institution seeks financial aid from the government in carrying out its own program—a grant is requested.

Sometimes, the distinction between grant and contract program is clouded. There may be useful assistance elements in contracts and procurement features in grants that otherwise provide grantee program assistance.

R.F.P.'s — the Request for a Proposal

The Request for a Proposal is a document prepared by a government agency that plans to contract for specific needed services or activities.

The R.F.P. usually includes a "work order" which is a description of the services required and defines certain criteria for the professional personnel needed. Due dates for submission of proposals are, of course, provided. Sometimes, the R.F.P. will contain information about personal conferences with the agency or announcement of a meeting with attendance of interested and qualified potential contractors invited for a general discussion of possible contracts.

Following is a typical example of an announcement of the availability of an R.F.P. from the National Institutes of Health, U.S. Department of Health, Education, and Welfare.

NIH GUIDE supplement — for GRANTS and CONTRACTS

U.S. DEPARTMENT OF HEALTH, EDUCATION, AND WELFARE

NIDR-4-75, August 16, 1974

ANNOUNCEMENT

RESEARCH STUDY TO DETERMINE THE EFFICACY OF
ANTIGENIC COMPONENTS IN ANTI-CARIES VACCINES

The National Institute of Dental Research plans to issue RFP No. NIH-NIDR-
2-75-4R for a research study on immunization against experimental dental
caries. To complement on-going studies which are utilizing enzyme vaccines
derived from cariogenic streptococci, this announcement requests efforts
directed toward use of antigens other than enzymes. Examples of such
antigens would be cell walls or cell membranes and extracts or fractions
derived therefrom. These antigens should be obtained from cariogenic
streptococci and should be devoid of transferase or other enzyme activity.

Experiments should be performed in rodent caries models in which previous
studies have confirmed the capability for inducing controlled experimental
dental caries.

The RFP package will be available approximately August 26. Proposals will
be due at NIDR no later than 60 days after the date of the RFP. Interested
sources who believe they are qualified to perform this work may request a
copy of the RFP. All requests must be in writing and submitted to the
following address:

> National Institutes of Health
> National Institute of Dental Research
> Office of Collaborative Research
> Room 557, Westwood Building
> Attention: Mrs. Edith Mullen
> Bethesda, Maryland   20014

PLEASE NOTE: A reasonable number of RFP's have been prepared and will be
issued upon receipt of a written request on an "as available" basis.

Announcements about available R.F.P.'s are mailed to lists of possible suppliers of services. Announcements from the National Institutes of Health would normally go to all medical and dental schools, and all teaching hospitals, and universities having graduate faculties with wide research capabilities. Any institution that receives a research or training grant from N.I.H. is periodically asked to report, on a form, those research areas for which it would be interested in receiving R.F.P. announcements.

The contracting process is more involved and complicated than handling grant awards and budgets. It is an aspect of government support that develops usually after an institution has had experience with grant projects. Most Federal agencies are reluctant to put an institution on the list to receive information about contract proposals, unless it already has a "track record" of successful grants management over a period of several years.

Acceptance of a contract implies a great degree of government supervision of operation and compliance with government policies on property records, employment practices, and accounting procedures. But, with all of this, it has its rewards, because, in many cases, the largest Federal grants come in the form of contracts. The policy objective is to arrive at a feasible and rational joint effort where the program purposes and goals of both contracting parties — the government and the grantee institution — are well served.

CHAPTER 4

Applications and Proposals

Applications and Grants—Proposals and Contracts

Under the current funding system of the U.S. Department of Health, Education, and Welfare, there are two clearly defined procedures for applying for and receiving Federal funds:

Applications — for grants or awards

Proposals — for contracts.

When seeking funds to support the ongoing program for your institutions, you go the grant route. If your plan is to offer services and staff of your agency to assist a government program, you go the contract route. A more complex institution may well be involved in both grants and contracts.

How do you decide, in the beginning, what method best suits your school, college, hospital, clinic, social agency, community group, or research institute?

As a general rule, if your agency is one of hundreds or thousands of similar programs in the community or country, you will use the project grant method of government support. If your institution has unique or special facilities, highly trained, specialized, scarce manpower resources, they may be in demand or needed by government agencies, and a contract can be developed to the mutual benefit of the institution and the government agency. In considering this possibility, it is important to evaluate the impact of a government contract on your own institutional program.

Does the staff have time to do the additional work?

Will use of your facilities, i.e., computer, atomic reactor, laboratories, office space, support services detract from your regular program?

Some agencies are planned to allow for government contracts as an integral part of their program, and necessary allowances are made for flexible staffs and sub-contracting to meet special requirements. However, probably 75% of the readers of this manual are associates with basic health, education, and social agencies with an inherent program objective which has primary claim on its resources. The opportunity for a government contract will be a special occasion indeed.

Applying for a Federal Grant

The Public Health Service of the U.S. Department of Health, Education, and Welfare has developed the most comprehensive and coherent grant application process, under its new *Grants Policy Statement* (DHEW Publication No. 05 74-50,000), which became effective on July 1, 1974. (A single copy of this manual may be requested from the Grants Inquiries Section, Division of Research Grants, National Institutes of Health, Bethesda, Maryland 20014.)

An examination of the PHS Grants Application Kit pinpoints the following key elements of applying for a grant.

1. *Deadlines for Submission:* Every Federal grant program, except National Science Foundation Research Grants, has a deadline date for submitting proposals. Applications for new or first time Research Grants from the National Institutes of Health have deadlines of October 1, February 1, and June 1.

What does this deadline mean? An application received by the October 1 deadline will receive a review and evaluation by panels of scientists over a four-month period. In the following March, it will be presented to the National Council of the Institute with recommendations for approval, deferral, rejection.

The Council will render its final recommendations, and, if approved, the grantee will be notified by May 1. The funds will most likely be available at the time of approval announcement.

Thus, at a minimum, there is a lead time span of seven months between submitting the grant application and receiving the grant award announcement. Add to this the time it takes for faculty or staff to prepare a high quality application — 1 month to 6 weeks. It is realistic to estimate almost a year — for the lead time requirement — to begin thinking seriously about applying for an N.I.H. research grant and the actual date of the grant award. This is the schedule for the largest and most important research grant program (in health and training, education and social field) in the Federal government. ($2.1 billion appropriated for the National Institutes of Health for fiscal year 1975.)

The following illustration — the front page from the application instruction sheet — provides a more complete picture of the application deadline system.

DEPARTMENT OF HEALTH, EDUCATION, AND WELFARE

PUBLIC HEALTH SERVICE

INFORMATION AND INSTRUCTIONS FOR APPLICATION FOR RESEARCH GRANT, FORM NIH 398
(Formerly PHS 398)

GENERAL INFORMATION

Follow instructions carefully. Lack of complete and relevant information may cause delay and misunderstanding in the review of your application.

Complete applications, including necessary signatures and appended materials, received before the following deadline dates will be reviewed during the months indicated. However, applicants are urged to submit their applications at any time during the year in order to avoid an undue concentration of applications on each deadline date. Late applications will normally be held for the next cycle of review. Deadlines may be waived at the discretion of the Chief, Research Grants Review Branch, Division of Research Grants, National Institutes of Health.

Information about the action on the grant application will be provided after council review. A principal investigator may obtain more detailed information concerning the critique of the proposal by submitting a request, in writing, to the staff member who signed the letter informing him of the council's action.

New and supplemental applications received by	Renewal applications received by	Presented to council in	Earliest probable beginning date of new projects
Oct. 1	Sept. 1	March	May 1
Feb. 1	Jan. 1	June	Sept. 1
June 1	May 1	November	Jan. 1

ASSURANCES REQUIRED FROM APPLICANT INSTITUTIONS. Before an award is made for an approved application, the institution must submit and have accepted an Assurance of Compliance with the Civil Rights Act of 1964. (Form HEW 441)

2. *Funding Periods:* An essential part of the application is, of course, the program budget. This means a request for a specific dollar amount to be spent over a given period of time, usually 12 months. Research grants have funding periods ranging from 6 months to 12 months, to 18 months to 2 and 3 years, depending on the scope of the project. But in no case will the Federal government award grants in larger than 12-month budgets. Funds for additional months or years will be committed in the original grant award.

Renewal or continuing applications must be prepared and submitted for each 12-month budget period for which a commitment has been made by the granting agency. It is understood from the first grant award that continued funding will be dependent upon continued appropriations from the U.S. Congress.

3. *Application Formats:* Most Federal grant programs have a regular grant application form to be used by the institution or agency applying for the grant.

A notable exception is the Grants for Scientific Research program of the National Science Foundation. NSF publishes a compact and complete booklet (Grants for Scientific Research NSF 73-12), which is, in fact, a very handy manual on how to draft a grant application. It takes the scientist step-by-step through the writing and preparation of the application, including sample application pages.

The actual NSF research grant application is to be typed on 8½" x 11" typing paper, according to the directions in the manual — *there is no printed form.*

Research grant applications for the National Institutes of Health must be made on the grant application provided by the Public Health Service grants office. The application form is actually part of a kit which includes an instruction sheet and complete information about regulations and guidelines for the research grant programs.

The next illustration is a copy of the "cover sheet" for the N.I.H. application. A careful study of this page will reveal some of the basic institutional arrangements which must be identified and involved in order to have a valid application.

Form Approved
Budget Bureau No. 68-R0240

DEPARTMENT OF
HEALTH, EDUCATION, AND WELFARE
PUBLIC HEALTH SERVICE

GRANT APPLICATION

	LEAVE BLANK	
TYPE	PROGRAM	NUMBER
REVIEW GROUP		FORMERLY
COUNCIL (Month, Year)		DATE RECEIVED

TO BE COMPLETED BY PRINCIPAL INVESTIGATOR (Items 1 through 7 and 15A)

1. TITLE OF PROPOSAL (Do not exceed 53 typewriter spaces)

2. PRINCIPAL INVESTIGATOR	3. DATES OF ENTIRE PROPOSED PROJECT PERIOD (This application)	
2A. NAME (Last, First, Initial)	FROM	THROUGH
2B. TITLE OF POSITION	**4. TOTAL DIRECT COSTS RE-QUESTED FOR PERIOD IN ITEM 3**	**5. DIRECT COSTS REQUESTED FOR FIRST 12-MONTH PERIOD**
2C. MAILING ADDRESS (Street, City, State, Zip Code)	**6. PERFORMANCE SITE(S)** (See Instructions)	

2D. DEGREE   **2E. SOCIAL SECURITY NO.**

2F. TELE-PHONE DATA | Area Code TELEPHONE NUMBER AND EXTENSION

2G. DEPARTMENT, SERVICE, LABORATORY OR EQUIVALENT (See Instructions)

2H. MAJOR SUBDIVISION (See Instructions)

7. Research Involving Human Subjects (See Instructions)

A. ☐ NO B. ☐ YES Approved: _____

C. ☐ YES – Pending Review _____ Date

8. Inventions (Renewal Applicants Only - See Instructions)

A. ☐ NO B. ☐ YES – Not previously reported

C. ☐ YES – Previously reported

TO BE COMPLETED BY RESPONSIBLE ADMINISTRATIVE AUTHORITY (Items 8 through 13 and 15B)

9. APPLICANT ORGANIZATION(S) (See Instructions)

11. TYPE OF ORGANIZATION (Check applicable item)

☐ FEDERAL ☐ STATE ☐ LOCAL ☐ OTHER (Specify)

12. NAME, TITLE, ADDRESS, AND TELEPHONE NUMBER OF OFFICIAL IN BUSINESS OFFICE WHO SHOULD ALSO BE NOTIFIED IF AN AWARD IS MADE

10. NAME, TITLE, AND TELEPHONE NUMBER OF OFFICIAL(S) SIGNING FOR APPLICANT ORGANIZATION(S)

Telephone Number _____

13. IDENTIFY ORGANIZATIONAL COMPONENT TO RECEIVE CREDIT FOR INSTITUTIONAL GRANT PURPOSES (See Instructions)

14. ENTITY NUMBER (Formerly PHS Account Number)

Telephone Number (s) _____

15. CERTIFICATION AND ACCEPTANCE. We, the undersigned, certify that the statements herein are true and complete to the best of our knowledge and accept, as to any grant awarded, the obligation to comply with Public Health Service terms and conditions in effect at the time of the award.

SIGNATURES (Signatures required on original copy only. Use ink, "Per" signatures not acceptable)	A. SIGNATURE OF PERSON NAMED IN ITEM 2A	DATE
	B. SIGNATURE(S) OF PERSON(S) NAMED IN ITEM 10	DATE

NIH 398 (FORMERLY PHS 398)
Rev. 1/73

Items on Cover Page

1.Title of Proposal: This suggests that the plan or write-up for the proposed scientific research project must have sufficient coherence to have a title.

2. Principal Investigator: This requirement means that a faculty or staff member with appropriate professional and scientific qualifications must be designated as project director. This person has primary responsibility for conduct of the research and preparation of scientific reports.

3. Dates for entire project period: This information necessitates a careful, rational plan for a research project that may be carried on for a 2- or 3-year period.

4. Total Direct Costs: This means that the planner must have the knowledge and capability to "cost out" the project and justify the costs in a way that will be understandable and reasonable to those who will evaluate the application.

9. Applicant Organization: The organization has to be one that has the qualifications and the criteria for eligibility for the grant.

10. Official signing for organization: Officer must be officially designated to sign an application on behalf of the applicant institution, i.e., university, hospital, clinic, etc. This signature, in effect, establishes an agreement to perform the research proposed and to account for the funds provided.

12. Official in Business Office: This officer is the person to whom checks will actually be sent and is presumed to be the official responsible for disbursing grant funds.

Information Required in the Body of the Application

A. Research objectives: This consists of a carefully and professionally constructed prose description of the proposed research project. It will perforce reveal a highly specialized understanding of the field of research and indicate by appropriate citations, awareness of all related research being done by others in the field.

B. Detailed budget and budget estimate: Categorical budget date (personnel, supplies, equipment, computer time etc., must be provided for the first 12-month period).

The following table is illustrative of the actual average budgets of research grants funded by the National Science Founddation over the last three years.

The average research grant budget for NSF grants has remained at $43,000 per annum for the last three years. In large budgets, the time and effort of professionals must be indicated for the dollar amounts requested, i.e., 1/3 time, 1/2 time, 2 summer months, etc.

SCIENTIFIC RESEARCH PROJECTS
AVERAGE DISTRIBUTION OF FUNDS BY TYPE OF EXPENDITURE

	Fiscal Year 1971		Fiscal Year 1972		Fiscal Year 1973	
	Amount	Percent of total	Amount	Percent of total	Amount	Percent of total
Professional Personnel						
Faculty	$ 6,560	15.0	$ 6,194	14.1	$ 6,506	14.9
Research Associates	2,668	6.1	2,987	6.8	3,342	7.7
Research Assistants	5,510	12.6	4,877	11.1	5,124	11.7
Other Professional	2,274	5.2	2,065	4.7	1,916	4.4
Total Professional Personnel	17,012	38.9	16,123	36.7	16,888	38.7
Other Personnel	3,499	8.0	3,383	7.7	3,342	7.6
Fringe Benefits	1,618	3.7	1,757	4.0	1,961	4.5
Total Salaries and Wages	**22,129**	**50.6**	**21,263**	**48.4**	**22,191**	**50.8**
Permanent Equipment	2,756	6.3	2,724	6.2	2,451	5.6
Expendable Equipment and Supplies	3,149	7.2	2,900	6.6	3,253	7.4
Travel	1,356	3.1	1,318	3.0	1,337	3.1
Publication Costs	612	1.4	615	1.4	668	1.5
Computer Costs	1,356	3.1	1,186	2.7	1,114	2.6
Other Costs	2,536	5.8	3,778	8.6	1,918	4.4
Total Direct Costs	**33,894**	**77.5**	**33,784**	**76.9**	**32,932**	**75.4**
Indirect Costs	9,840	22.5	10,148	23.1	10,739	24.6
Total Average Grant	**$43,734**	**100.0**	**$43,932**	**100.0**	**$43,671**	**100.0**

Who Should Draft a Grant Application?

One of the most prevalent mythologies about the grant application process is that drafting an application requires unique skills and talents possessed by a select company of grant specialists.

Applications for government grants, at the present state of the art, are practically self-executing in their format and requirements. They are designed so as to require that the faculty or professional staff person who will actually direct the project must write up the application. This situation practically rules out the practice of special proposal writers. Government cost regulations actually prohibit including in a grant application budget any cost incurred in preparing the application.

There are some exceptions to this procedure. For special "one-time" applications such as facilities grants for hospitals or colleges or long-term environmental studies projects for the Environmental Protection Agency, to give just two examples, it would be feasible to retain special consultants to assist in preparing the application. In the case of facilities applications, the architects of necessity must be involved to draft the specifications for the building.

The decision on who will draft the application is one that belongs, I believe with the office that has been given institutional responsibility for coordinating and managing the government grant process.

On occasion, the development office (fund raising and public relations) is proposed as the responsible unit for writing applications and proposals for government grants. This is assumed because a development office may have had success with private foundation proposals. But development staff involvement in government grant applications could be risky.

The surest rule to follow is that faculty, scientists, or other professional staff who would direct the project, if the grant is awarded, have primary responsibility for preparation of grant applications and proposals.

The Peer Review Process

What happens to a grant application after it has been carefully prepared and put in the mail (or sometimes hand-carried) in advance of the required deadline for submission?

It goes through an evaluation process at the granting agency. At the National Institutes of Health, each research or training application receives what amounts to a three-tiered review and evaluation, which results in a decision to award or not award — or sometimes to defer a grant.

This complex and highly regarded system is known generally as the "peer review process." The three levels of review include the following:

1. Agency staff study and checking; This involves the professional staff of the particular institute.

2. Study Sections: These are committees of scientists, professors, and professionals who serve for four years and provide detailed professional analysis of applications and the research, manpower, and resources proposed for funding support.

3. National Council: This is a prestigious, statutorily required advisory board of senior scientists in the areas of the various institutes, i.e., Cancer, Heart, Mental Health, etc.

All of the above three review stages are undertaken by persons who are professional peers of the applicants. That is, they are presumed to be knowledgeable about the professional and research competence of the applicant because, in a sense, they are all colleagues; hence, the term "peer process."

Thus, it is understandable why it is absolutely necessary to have a Federal grant application prepared by some person who is a professional or scientific peer of the people who will be evaluating the application.

The acceptable scientific, professional, or program write-up for the application must reflect this concept by appropriate references to and footnoting to the latest literature in the proposed field of research or educational activity.

The accompanying curriculum vitae of the staff listed on the application must reveal their professional experience and status. (How detailed the curriculum vitae can and should be is illustrated in Chapter IX.) The bibliographies of the staff publications — a complete list of all books, articles, and addresses ever presented — must be included. This will also indicate the standing of the persons proposing the application which can then be judged by their professional peers.

Grant Application Institutional Approval

The final step before submitting the grant application to the granting agency is to provide for official institutional approval. Functionally, this is a simple procedure, requiring only that the authorized official of the institution sign and date the application on behalf of the submitter.

But it is at this point that the budget for the grant should receive a careful review and analysis by the institution's official. The grant will legally be made to the institution — its corporate entity, which will be held responsible by the Federal (or State and City) government for spending the funds granted, according to the grant budget as approved and the program as proposed.

For the budget and other institutional aspects of a grant application, it is feasible to have specialists who assist the faculty or other professionals. Most successful grant getting institutions have staff who become very knowledgeable about writing up grant budgets and negotiating with granting agencies on matters of both direct and indirect costs for the project proposed.

A successful effort will involve a close and trusting collaboration between the staff who develop and would operate the program for which the grant is received and the technical staff who would participate in the financial management of the grant, including preparation of the budget.

This often delicate and diplomatic task, should be under the careful and firm control of the grant officer of the institution.

Finally, I would affirm with whatever force that printed word can muster that the best way to learn how to prepare successful government grant applications is to start doing it.

Pick out the programs that are appropriate for your institution, find staff who can write up the program, work out a budget, and send it in. But follow the application instructions to the last detail!

CHAPTER 5

Financial Aspects of Sponsored Programs

Defining Institutional Policies for Fiscal Management of Grant and Contract Budgets

Accountability is the keynote of the fiscal management requirements for government grant programs.

Accountability begins with the preparation of the budget for a grant or contract application or proposal and ends with the final "report of expenditures," which is submitted to the granting agency within 90 days after the end of the budget period for the grant. Beyond this, many contracts require that the grantee keep financial records available for up to six years, to be examined by government auditors.

Annual reports of expenditures are the usual requirements for most Federal project grants. Certain Federal programs which provide for payment of stipends to students or trainees, for example, may have a requirement for the grantee to obtain a special audit — from a public accounting firm. Cost for such a requirement is covered by an allotment of funds for the audit in the grant budget.

Financial Report Requirements for State and Local Government Grants

Most grants from state and local governments are "cost reimbursable" contracts. This means that, in order to get payment for the grant, an expenditure report must be provided to the state agency for project costs incurred — say, for the previous monthly or quarterly period. This is common practice with New York State agencies, even when they are making grants from Federal funds which they already have in hand.

The Program Budget Concept

All government grant programs now operate under the program budget plan. This means that a detailed budget is prepared as part of the educational, health, social service, etc. project plan — as part of the application. Dollar costs for all aspects of the project must be developed and justified. Once the grant is awarded, expenditures are made in accordance with the budget. Variations are permitted, within reasonable limits, and with permission in writing from a project officer at the granting agency.

This may sound very complicated and time-consuming. But as an institution becomes active in the grant process, these accounting activities develop a routine of their own.

I believe it is accurate to state that Federal grant programs are the best managed and accounted for in the whole grant field. Federal management guidelines are feasible and reasonable, and Federal project managers are invariably helpful and cooperative. They are always available to take phone calls or questions about use of grant funds and can usually assist in unraveling knotty problems on the spot.

Incentives for Good Grants Management

Centralizing responsibility and authority for grants management in the grantee institution is the basis for keeping control of the financial aspects of grants and for maintaining the accountability referred to above.

The incentive and motivation formula is strongly recommended. How does it work? There are four touchstones of accountability in the fiscal management of grants:

1. The signature of the official representative, on behalf of the institution, in submitting applications and proposals.

2. Setting up the grant account after an award has been made and the review and approval of expenditures from the account.

3. Disbursement of funds after an expenditure has been approved.

4. Preparation of financial reports.

The key elements in the accountability system are #2 and #4, assuring that expenditures from grants are made according to the provisions of the budget and the task of preparing financial reports.

The authority to sign proposals and applications and to disburse funds have a certain prestige and status. By linking the authority for proposal signing with the responsibility for reviewing grant expenditures and preparing financial reports, a motivation and incentive for careful and effective management of grant funds is significantly enhanced.

I believe it is imperative for one designated institutional official to be responsible for all three functions. Finally, if the same official's name appears on both the *application* and the grant's *financial report,* the granting institution has a sense of confidence that fiscal management is consistent and coherent.

Actual disbursement of grant funds can be efficiently assigned to another institutional officer, usually the Controller or Treasurer, or a member of the Finance Office staff. This office can serve as an alternate internal check on grant administration. But care should be taken so that the internal check does not become a delaying factor or an opportunity for internal bureaucratic rivalry interfering with the smooth execution of the project.

Occasionally, the head of the institution will perceive it as his prerogotive to sign all proposals for grants. If this procedure should be enforced, it should only be a formality and undertaken after review and checking of the proposal and budget by the official that will have responsibility for fiscal management of the grant. Of course, in an institution with a modest grant load (i.e., no more than 5 or 6 a year), the chief executive officer could take on the task of proposal review for submission and directly supervise grant expenditures from that office.

Grants management has a double objective, each of equal importance: expenditure of grant funds according to the guidelines and policies of both the granting agency and the grantee institution, and providing fiscal management services to the professional staff who are directing the grant project. The professional project director must also be involved in the process. The most direct way to do this is to require the project director to personally sign off on every expenditure for a grant. This responsibility cannot be avoided. Some professionals, scientists, professors, doctors will resist involvement in accounting for expenditures on their grants. They will take the position that they don't have time to be bothered with financial matters. But a total accountability concept will not leave out the project director.

When the project director is adequately serviced with monthly expenditure reports on the grant and expenditure requests are swiftly and accurately executed, confidence and assurance will develop.

Provisions by an institution for a rational, simple, fiscal management system for government grants is a basic motivating factor in encouraging professional staff to continue to seek and prepare grant applications.

Government Agency Requirements for Grants Management*

The bible of government grant directors is popularly referred to as OMB Circular A-21. This title refers to a standing memorandum from the Office of Management and Budget of the Executive Office of the President. It is the basic Federal guideline for determining costs applicable to research and development and educational services under grants and contracts with educational institutions.

However, the cost principles used in A-21 have been incorporated into the guidelines and procedures for all Federal grant programs.

The Department of Health, Education and Welfare pub-

* Material in this section is based on the following documents: *Direct and Indirect Costs of Research at College and Universities.* Published by Commission on Federal Relations, American Council on Education.
Circular No. A-21, Office of Management & Budget, Sept. 2, 1970, Washington, D.C.

lished a comprehensive *Grants Administration Manual,* which incorporates the provisions of A-21. Any person assigned responsibility for government grants should secure a copy of the Manual and study it carefully before ever looking at a grant application.

This chapter is not intended to provide a detailed analysis of Circular A-21. But it will be helpful to get an overview of the costs concept involved in making grant budgets.

Cost Principles for Government Grants

One of the first questions that is asked when administrators or staff plan for government grants or undertake proposals is: What will the grant pay for? The answer is simple.

The grant will pay for the cost of the project. According to A-21, the costs under a Federally sponsored research grant or contract include: 1) all those expenses that have been incurred solely for work on the project (direct costs), and 2) a share of those other costs that are incurred primarily for necessary supporting administrative and service functions related to the sponsored project (indirect costs). When these two classes of expenditures have been determined, using the principles set forth in Circular A-21, they must be added to obtain the total costs of the project.

Direct costs usually include the following kinds of costs:

Personnel costs: *Salaries and Wages* of staff fully employed on the project and a percentage of the salaries of those working part-time in proportion to their efforts on the project. *Personnel Benefits:* fringe benefits such as Social Security, retirement, health benefits, etc.

Supplies: Consumable supplies needed exclusively for the project.

Travel and
Communication: All charges that are directly incurred for the project.

Equipment: Usually, the cost of equipment acquired for specific use in the project, as set forth in the terms of the grant or contract.

Computer Use and Alterations and renovations of space directly related to a project can also be included as a direct cost.

Indirect Costs, generally cover the following categories of institutional supporting activities.

General Administration and General Expense: Accounting, payroll, administrative offices, etc.

Research and Grant Administration: Personnel and other costs of offices whose responsibility is the administration of research.

Plant Operation and Maintenance: Utilities, janitorial services, routine maintenance and repairs.

Library Expense: Books, library staff.

Departmental Administrative Expenses: Administrative costs for the various program divisions of the institution.

Depreciation or Use Allowance: For buildings and equipment, excluding those paid for by the Federal government.

Some institutional costs may be classified as either direct or indirect costs, depending on how the institution organizes its business and administrative affairs. Examples include the following:

Secretarial services; Social Security, retirement contributions, and group insurance, hospitalization, and medical benefits; Postage and communications (both local and long distance telephone calls); Office equipment — including typewriters and calculating machines.

A basic rule to follow is to accept the fact that a given cost factor cannot be both a direct and indirect cost at the same time. A typical example of this category is *fringe benefits.* Many institutions have the total fringe benefit package built into the "general expense" cost of the institution. Under this category, fringe benefits are calculated as an aspect of indirect costs.

But when a grant is awarded and specific full-time grant personnel are appointed, the institution's Personnel Office will question providing full fringe benefits for the grant personnel. The real cost of fringe benefits for the special personnel looms large. But this type of policy should always be determined in advance.

When an institution is new to the Federal grant process, the indirect cost rate is initially a provisional determination. After the institution has had a Federal audit of its grant activity, the government auditors will work with the institution to determine a permanent indirect cost rate — to serve until the next Federal audit — usually three years.

Finally, it should be understood that the indirect cost element of a grant budget is not a profit or net income to the institution. It is a dollar amount that represents a ratio of the cost of the institution's general administration and supporting continuing costs as compared to the specific costs of a specific service or activity of the institution. Indirect cost rates usually range from 40% to 60% of the salaries and wages part of a grant budget. This budget item goes into the general fund of the institution and grant project directors have no special claim to these funds.

Cost-Sharing

For the last several years, the U.S. Congress has provided for a cost-sharing requirement in all Federally funded research grants, when enacting the appropriation bills which provide funds for these grant programs.

The minimum is 5% of total project costs. This means that the grantee institution must share an equivalent cost of the project. This can be done by cost-sharing out of the indirect cost allotment in the grant or by providing an equivalent service of materials to the project from institutional personnel or services, or equipment. This latter method of cost-sharing can be covered by having the project director contribute extra time to the project, or provision for computer services, secretarial services (if not covered by indirect costs), or by providing access to special equipment, etc. In any case, the direct cost-sharing must be accounted for in the financial report of expenditures and must be documented in some acceptable fashion in the grantee institution's records.

In conclusion, I would advise, as I have on other aspects of grant activity, that the handling of indirect costs and cost-sharing is a part of the grant process that one can only learn by actually going through the work.

In order to get a concrete idea of the scope of the costs allowed in government grants, I am reprinting the list of 45 items that form the basis for general standards for costing in grant budgets.

GENERAL STANDARDS FOR
SELECTED ITEMS OF COST

1. Advertising costs
2. Bad debts
3. Capital expenditures
4. Civil defense costs
5. Commencement and convocation costs
6. Communication costs
7. Compensation for personal services
8. Contingency provisions
9. Deans of faculty and graduate schools
10. Depreciation and use allowances
11. Employee morale, health and welfare costs and credits
12. Entertainment costs
13. Equipment and other facilities
14. Fines and penalties
15. Insurance and indemnification
16. Interest, fund raising, and investment management costs
17. Labor relations costs
18. Losses on other research agreements or contracts
19. Maintenance and repair costs
20. Material costs
21. Memberships, subscriptions and professional activity costs
22. Patent costs
23. Pension plan costs
24. Plant security costs
25. Preresearch agreement costs
26. Professional services costs
27. Profits and losses on disposition of plant, equipment or other capital assets
28. Proposal costs

29. Public information services costs
30. Rearrangement and alteration costs
31. Reconversion costs
32. Recruiting costs
33. Royalties and other costs for use of patents
34. Sabbatical leave costs
35. Scholarships and student aid costs
36. Severance pay
37. Specialized service facilities operated by institution
38. Special services costs
39. Staff benefits
40. Student activity costs
41. Student services costs
42. Taxes
43. Transportation costs
44. Travel costs
45. Termination costs applicable to research agreements.

Grant Budget-Making

The best single publication on how to write a proposal is the National Science Foundation's basic manual entitled *Grants For Scientific Research.* (Single copies are available from the NSF, Washington, D.C. 20550.)

As indicated by the NSF guidelines, proposal making is essentially a three-part job.

1. A decision must be made as to the type of research, training, or other program activity for which project support is sought.

2. Who, when, where, and what to submit must be determined. The principal investigator or potential project

director must prepare the research or program aspects of the proposal.

3. The budget is then developed on the basis of the work outlined in the project description.

For the typical research grant budget, a close collaboration is needed between the professional person, the potential project director, and the budget analyst in the grants or finance office of the institution.

Research Grant Budgets

Nobody but the project director could write up the project description. But an experienced budget officer can be most helpful to a scientist or other professional in costing out the budget for a proposal.

Thus, one of the most useful institutional services to be provided staff in connection with grant applications is budget assistance.

The following budget categories are the typical model budget items for a research grant:

A.   SALARIES AND WAGES:

1.   Senior Personnel:
   a.   (Co) Principal Investigator
        (list by name)
   b.   Faculty Associates
        (list by name)

2.   Other Personnel (Non-faculty)
   a.   Research Assoc. (Post-doctoral)
        (list separately by name if available; otherwise give numbers)

      b. Non-Fac. Professionals (Other)
          (list separately by category, giving number, e.g., one computer programmer)
      c. (number) Grad. Students (Res. Asst.)
      d. (number) Pre-Baccalaureate Students
      e. (number) Secretarial-Clerical
      f. (number) Technical, Shop & Other

B. STAFF BENEFITS

C. TOTAL SALARIES, WAGES AND STAFF BENEFITS (A + B)

D. PERMANENT EQUIPMENT:
    (list as required)

E. EXPENDABLE SUPPLIES AND EQUIPMENT:

F. TRAVEL:
    1. Domestic
    2. Foreign
       (list as required)

G. PUBLICATION COSTS

H. COMPUTER COSTS

I. OTHER COSTS (itemize by major type)

J. TOTAL DIRECT COSTS (C through I)

K. INDIRECT COSTS:
    1. On Campus . . . . % of . . . . . .
    2. Off Campus . . . . % of . . . . . .

L. TOTAL COSTS (J plus K)

M. TOTAL CONTRIBUTIONS FROM OTHER
    SOURCES

N. TOTAL ESTIMATED PROJECT COST . . . .

Training Grant Budgets

The layout of costs for a training (teaching, services, technical assistance) grant is identical to the research grant pattern. There are some alternative expenditures and costs which might be included.

Faculty and teaching assistants would be listed as teaching personnel — in the Personnel section of the budget.

Stipends for trainees is another common training grant item.

Tuition for courses provided is still another possible training grant budget item.

Fees for special health or welfare services could be provided in service grants.

Additional Income for Staff

Under present Federal regulations, it is not possible to build in additional or supplementary salary income for regular staff of the grant recipient.

Faculty, staff, and other professionals' salaries are supported from the grant, for that portion of the regular professional time and effort allocated to the project, at the same rate of salary as the assigned institutional base salary for the fiscal year in which the grant is operative.

Because of this policy, many institutions now take into account present or potential grant support when assigning or negotiating salaries and total compensation for their professional staff.

The only exception, allowing "overtime" pay from grants (on Federal programs) is for educational service awards, and the basis for the overtime must be justified in the application. The Federal government accepts the possibility that certain busy and key teachers may be needed for a project, but cannot be relieved of their regular teaching assignments. If all parties are in agreement, they can be used on an overload basis, and be so reimbursed from the grant. This policy is also followed for special medical and other health personnel in certain service agreements.

In conclusion, I wish to reaffirm the importance of the clear and definite assignment of fiscal management responsibility in any institution desiring to get government grants. The authority

☐ to review and officially sign proposals;

☐ to establish grant budgets and review grant expenditures;

☐ and the responsibility to prepare financial reports on grant expenditures

should be under the jurisdiction of, or at a minimum, be coordinated by a single institutional officer.

Anything less will not satisfy the requirements of the granting agencies or meet the needs of an institution which needs and is entitled to participate in government grant programs.

CHAPTER 6

Government Grant Reporting

"Accountability" was the keynote for the review and analysis of systems for financial management of government grants in the previous chapter.

It is the requirement for final reports, both *technical* and *financial*, however, that usually presents the greatest accountability challenge to an institution, as it moves into government grant programming.

Invariably, the initial reception of government grants generates a great deal of excitement and anticipation throughout the whole organization. Trustees and board members are pleased. A new source of financial support has been tapped. The chief administrator feels a new sense of pride in the staff. He can now boast or casually mention, depending on his style, of getting grants from N.I.H., or the National Science Foundation, or H.E.W., etc. when he is meeting with his fellow administrators at national conferences. His college, or hospital, or social service agency has "joined the club."

Proudest of all will be the professional staff person who is the designated project director for the grant. This euphoria will be shared with immediate colleagues and assistants who may be receiving support for their work from grant funds.

The only people in the institution taking a dim view of the matter might be the staff of the financial office who are vaguely aware of the new necessity for meticulous financial reports while the project is under way and after it is finished. They will have heard about this chore from colleagues at professional meetings of their own.

Thus, the need for a clear understanding of the responsibility for reporting — before and after the fact of the application for the grant — and the arrival of the grant award announcement when you can begin to spend the funds.

Program and Technical Reporting

The technical or progress report is the responsibility of the project director or principal investigator. This is the individual designated by the grantee and approved by the granting agency who will be responsible for the scientific, professional, or technical direction of the project. The term "Principal Investigator" generally is used in basic research projects, while the term "Project Director" generally is used in educational, service, or other program projects.

The technical report required by the grant sponsors may be provided for in two ways: a formal report — or publication in professional journals.

A formal report, in narrative form, with appropriate scientific and other data must be prepared and a requisite number of copies forwarded to the granting agency within a time limit prescribed by the sponsor. If the grant supported a service program, rosters of all persons receiving instruction or special training or treatment are sometimes required. The various outcomes of the instruction or service must be documented in some appropriate fashion. Were degrees earned? Courses completed? Counseling provided — clinical treatment offered, etc.?

The problem for the institution is to make sure that the required report is prepared and submitted. Usually, because of its technical nature, only the professional staff is capable of doing the job. Generally, if the report is delinquent, the final payment towards the grant budget is withheld until the report is received.

As an alternative to a formal report, a *summary report* of research in progress or completed may be all that is required. It is understood by the sponsor, from the information provided in the application, that the research or other activity funded by the grant will be reported in various publications and journals or even result in the publication of a book.

Reporting Through Publication

The incentive and motivation for technical reports is built into the research grant system. As part of an application, a scientist must demonstrate that he has already "published" results of his research in professional journals, at a minimum. Other forms of publication and dissemination include papers read at professional meetings, articles prepared for more popular publications, and books or chapters in books.

The junior scientist demonstrates his capacity to report by indicating his participation in research reported by his professors or mentors, or senior colleagues, which reports he may have indeed written himself. The primary motivation for technical reporting is the absolute requirement for published evidence of research done on a grant, as a basis for application for a subsequent grant.

The more articles published or scientific papers presented and listed as part of a grant application, the better the chances for the grant to be approved. Of course, quantity is not the only criteria, although this charge has been frequently made.

This requirement for previously published research or other grant activity, as a basis for a grant application, leads to a strategic suggestion for an institution desiring to get into the grant field.

What do you do if none of the current professional staff has recently published grant reports to be used as a basis for new grant applications?

One possibility is to begin funding publishable research for qualified members of your staff out of the institution's own funds. Establish an in-house research grant program. It should be clear from the beginning that the in-house grants are seed money to enable staff to launch research activity that will lead to outside funding.

The other path of action is to employ new staff with demonstrated capacity to do sponsored research or get grant support for their professional work.

The publication of results and dissemination of new ideas and programs, as a result of a grant, are essential and crucial parts of the whole grant process.

Financial Reporting

In commenting on the financial reporting aspects of government grants, I am stressing the organization of the process and the nature of the requirements. The intent is to let readers know "what they are in for." The Federal agencies supply grantees with rationally designed financial report forms which are really quite simple to fill out, providing you have the necessary financial management system in place.

Comprehensive and coherent grant administration manuals are available from both H.E.W. and the National Science Foundation to serve as detailed guides on preparing necessary reports. Of course, this means that you have a grants office in your institution which will become knowledgeable about this prodecure and will command the necessary staff support and authority to carry out the reporting requirements.

Fixing Responsibility for Financial Reports

Properly designating responsibility for preparing financial reports is basic to achieving two important objectives in grant activity:

A) Getting the report prepared — and on time;

B) Assuring the professional staff that the financial aspects of their grant are being properly handled. Freeing them of any anxiety about this aspect of the program is a motivating factor in stimulating grant applications.

As has been recommended earlier, there are sound managerial arguments for assigning responsibility for preparing financial reports to the same office that has responsibility and authority to sign a proposal or application. In the NSF Grant Administration Manual, this official is defined in the following way:

Authorized Institutional Representative — the administrative official who is empowered to commit the proposing organization to the conduct of a project if NSF agrees to support it and who, by his signature on the proposal, is responsible for the prudent administration of the grant by the grantee institution, if NSF awards a grant.

Another official name, but not signature, is required on a grant application, defined as follows:

Business Officer—the financial official of the grantee institution who has primary responsibility for the accountability for and reporting on NSF grant funds. Thus, a grantee organization has an option here to centralize responsibility for grant approval, administration, and financial reporting, in one or two administrative officials. Both alternatives can work effectively and do, in different institutions.

In a relatively small institution, with no more than a dozen Federal grants in place in a given fiscal year, I believe it is quite feasible to assign responsibility for disbursement of grant funds and financial reports to the Business Office. The approval for submission of grant applications can be co-ordinated in another more academically or scientifically oriented administrator, who will be working with the project director.

But at all costs, it is imperative that, whatever option the institution chooses, grant submission, grant expenditure approval, and grant financial reports be under the control of one administrative official. To do otherwise is to invite an endless variety of hassels within the institution and also with granting agencies. Nothing is more likely to inhibit your institution or discourage the staff from getting grants. It is of the nature of Controllers and Financial Officers to exercise control of program operations on an organization-wide basis. The most powerful motivation for staff to get government grants is to have funds for their work, which they control. Agreed, that sponsored programs must fit into an institution's concerns and purposes. But the fiscal management of them should not result in a situation where the project directors perceive it thusly: "I did all the work in preparing the proposal; it's my professional competence that is being supported; I designed a budget to meet scientific requirements and I will spend the funds as they were approved by the granting agency" — only to be subjected to surveillance by a financial office that "nitpicks" expenditures of grant funds or insists on making interpretations of grant budgets that impinge on the professional aspects of the project, as the principal investigator sees it.

What the situation requires, in my opinion, is the provision of an administrative officer situated between the project director and the financial officer. The official should be perceived as an advocate and protector of the project director, on the one hand; but must also be accepted by the financial administrator, as one who will accept responsibility for reviewing the project director's requests for grant funds in conformity with approved grant budgets and the institution's own procedures for assuring accountability for proper disbursement and accounting of funds. This kind of even-handed administration and support for government grant programs is one of the most important elements in getting and increasing government grants.

The financial report form in the following illustration is provided by the Department of Health, Education, and Welfare, for final fiscal reports. The information requested is typical of that required by Federal granting agencies.

(All comments in this Chapter are based on provisions in the NSF Grant Administration Manual, October 1973, NSF, Washington, D.C. 20550.) (NSF Publication 73-26)

Department of Health, Education, and Welfare

	Grant No.
NAME AND ADDRESS OF GRANTEE INSTITUTION	DATE OF THIS REPORTING PERIOD
	TRANSACTION NO.
	FROM TO
	PROJECT PERIOD
	INSTITUTIONAL ID NO.
	FROM TO
	☐ CHECK IF FINAL REPORT

1. Expenditures of DHEW Funds for this Report Period

a. Personnel	$	h. Alterations and renovations	
b. Consultant services		i. Other	
c. Equipment			
d. Supplies		j. Total direct costs	
e. Travel, domestic		k. Indirect costs: Rate _____ % ☐ S&W ☐ TDC	
f. Travel, foreign		Base $ _____	
g. Patient care costs		l. TOTAL	$

2. Expenditures from Prior Periods (previously reported)	
3. Cumulative Expenditures	
4. Total Amount Awarded - Cumulatively	
5. Unexpended Balance (Item 4 less Item 3)	
6. Unliquidated Obligations	
7. Unobligated Balance (Item 5 less Item 6)	
8.a. Cost Sharing Information - Grantee Contribution This Period	
b. % of Total Project Costs (Item 8a divided by total of Items 1 and 8a)	%
9.a. Interest / Income (enclose check)	
b. Other Refundable Income (enclose check)	

10. Remarks

I hereby certify that this report is true and correct to the best of my knowledge, and that all expenditures reported herein have been made in accordance with appropriate grant policies and for the purposes set forth in the application and award documents.

_____
SIGNATURE OF INSTITUTION OFFICER   DATE

**REPORT OF RESEARCH GRANT
EXPENDITURES**

BUDGET BUREAU NO. 122-R0119

A few comments on the information requested are of interest. Item 8 calls for both a dollar amount and a percentage of project cost report on cost-sharing in the project by the grantee institution. This requirement was noted in Chapter 5.

Item 9a requests data on any interest earned from grant funds on deposit in the grantee institution. Federal regulations prohibit the grantee from getting interest income from grants.

These fiscal reporting requirements are illustrative of the fact that Federal grants are not profit-making gifts to the institution. They are not designed to support the ongoing program already in operation. They are not supposed to supplant institutional funds. I like to view them as "add-ons" and very significant because they are based on determined community and national needs and priorities.

Reporting On Cost-Reimbursable Contracts

The usual procedure for grants from State and local government agencies is by contract. The contract provides for financial reimbursement on the basis of submitted monthly, quarterly, or even annual expenditure reports. This system requires advance-funding of grant operations out of institutional funds. It also requires an ability to come up with expenditure data more rapidly.

Institutions are advised to carefully consider all the implications of these requirements. For example, advance funding is a cost in that it is actually a "loan" to the grant project. Reasonable interest charges for this cannot be built into the total project cost.

If your institution has a cash flow problem, a government contract may be a real liability. In any case, allowance for the funding of a grant must be planned and provided for.

Grant Payment Requests

Often overlooked is the clarification of responsibility for preparing payment requests. Who bills the granting agency for the funds? I have already described the system of reimbursement of costs based on submission of monthly or periodic expenditure reports. When this system is required, by a grant or contract agreement, usually, the check arrives in due course after the expenditure report is submitted.

Federal grant payments are made in advance, either through a *letter of credit* or a *treasury check*.

The letter of credit method is possible when an institution has a minimum of $250,000 annual grant total, from such agencies as the National Science Foundation or the National Institutes of Health. When grant funding reaches this level, the institutions negotiate this arrangement, through the agencies' financial management office. The grantee financial office submits a consolidated monthly estimate for all grants, and a check is forthcoming from the regional Federal Reserve Bank.

The cash advance system is used for smaller levels of funding. Arrangements can be made with the financial management office of the granting agency for treasury checks on a monthly, bi-weekly, or other regular cycle, or as required. Amounts for advances must be those necessary to meet the current disbursement needs of grantees.

Grant award announcements include complete information on how to apply for payments. The grantee institution should be sure about who is to prepare the bill.

The Auditing Process

Getting Federal grants results in becoming involved in the Federal audit process. The audit division of the Department of Health, Education, and Welfare now has responsibility for most educational, health, and social service institutions receiving Federal grants.

The most important basis for undergoing a successful audit is to have a system of grant and project files available for review by the auditors.

The grant file elements necessary for the audit include the following:

1. grant proposal or application.

2. grant award announcement.

3. institutional grant budget, incorporating the grant award.

4. records of all grant expenditures—including authorization by project directors, review by institutional officer, and disbursement report. These records will include copies of vouchers, bills, and payments requests which served as a basis for all expenditures.

If these four elements of grant records check out, the audit will be successful. That is, the auditors will report that grant funds were spent in accordance with the grant budget and program plans and that there was satisfactory evidence on file for these expenditures. This common-sense objective can have its complications. It is not within the scope of this chapter to analyze all of these.

Communicating With Auditors

The successful audit is based on a policy of maintaining complete and accurate records and full disclosure of these to the auditors.

There are two general rules to recommend for effective grantee-audit relationships.

1. When the auditors question grant expenditures relating to the purpose of the grant, bring in the project director to respond and explain.

2. If the audit report takes an exception to grant expenditures, involve the project director and the principal grants officer in preparing the formal reply. This task should never be left solely to a business or financial officer.

It can happen that both the auditor and the institutional business officer will not understand the program justification for certain expenditures. When the project director presents his professional justification, it has a much better chance of being understood and accepted by the grant program officer in the granting agency. Under current Federal audit practice, the Federal government is guided by program people in the agencies in final determination of any audit questions.

Federal grants management, including the reporting function, is the fastest new professional specialty in the United States today. I believe Federal grants are here to stay. Government support of privately controlled and funded programs in health, education and welfare is now built into the U.S. system.

As a summary of this demanding and formidable component of the grants process, I am including a glossary of terms most commonly used in identifying the essential personnel and procedures involved.

Authorized Institutional Representative — The administrative official who is empowered to commit the proposing organization to the conduct of a project if NSF agrees to support it and who, by his signature on the proposal, is responsible for the prudent administration of the grant by the grantee institution if NSF awards a grant.

Business Officer —The financial official of the grantee who has primary responsibility for the accountability for and reporting on NSF grant funds.

Consortium Grant — A master grant to one institution or organization in support of a project which is being carried out through a cooperative arrangement between or among the grantee and one or more other academic institutions or nonprofit organizations which are legally independent of the grantee.

Effective Date — The date the grant letter is signed by NSF unless some other effective date is specified therein. This date remains constant except under exceptional circumstances justifying a formal amendment to the grant letter. Allowable project costs may be charged against the grant on and after such date.

Expiration Date — The date specified in the grant letter after which expenditures may not be charged against the grant except to satisfy obligations of funds to pay allowable project costs committed on or before that date. NSF grants no longer contain a semi-automatic "grace period" following the expiration of an approximate grant period. The expiration date normally is the last day of the month.

Flexibility Period — NSF continues to recognize the need for flexibility in the amount of time needed to organize and conduct many types of research projects. In lieu of a "grace period," many NSF grants now incorporate a "flexibility period" of up to six months which terminates with the assigned expiration date.

Grant Period — The grant period extends from the effective date through the expiration date. In those NSF grants which do not include a flexibility period, the grant period is the same as the support period. In those which do include a flexibility period, the grant period is up to six months longer than the support period.

Grantee — The educational institution, hospital, public agency, or other organization which submits a proposal and receives a grant for support of a project under the direction of a named Principal Investigator or Project Director.

Grants Manager — NSF Grants and Contracts Office employee responsible for the policy and administration aspects of grant administration and for liaison with grantees in specific geographic areas.

Grants Officer — The official authorized by the Director, NSF, to take final action of NSF grants.

Principal Investigator (PI)/Project Director (PD) — The individual designated by the grantee and approved by NSF who will be responsible for the scientific or technical direction of the project. The term "Principal Investigator" generally is used in basic research projects, while the term "Project Director" generally is used in science education and other projects.

Prior NSF Approval — When such approval is called for, it may be granted either in the grant instrument (normally by reference in the grant budget to a request in the proposal) or by subsequent NSF correspondence. If not approved in the grant instrument, written request for such action, usually initiated by the PI or PD, should be signed or countersigned by the Authorized Institutional Representative and addressed to the cognizant Program Office, with a copy to the Grants and Contracts Office. Prior to the performance of the act, the Authorized Institutional Representative and the PI or PD must be in receipt of an approval letter.

Program Officer — The NSF scientific or technical employee responsible for evaluation of proposals and recommendation of action thereon in a specific area and, if an award is made, for the scientific aspects of grant administration and for liaison with Principal Investigators/Project Directors. The Program Office is identified in each award both in the Grant Budget and in the Project Summary, although the name of the individual Program Officer is not. The *OMB Catalog of Federal Domestic Assistance* and the NSF *Guide to Programs* identify most NSF Program Offices but not individual program officers.

Project — The activity outlined in the proposal and approved by NSF for support.

Proposal — The application for NSF support of a specific activity as outlined in the applicable NSF brochure or program announcement.

Senior Personnel —Those professorial or professional personnel who either are (1) responsible for the scientific or technical direction of an NSF-supported project as named Principal Investigators or Project Directors, or (2) senior assistants to the PI/PD. At academic institutions the senior personnel category includes faculty associates, but excludes research associates or research assistants. At either academic or nonacademic organizations, the category may include such scientists, engineers, physicians, or other professional personnel as NSF and the grantee agree should be considered senior personnel.

CHAPTER 7

Organizing Grant Operations

Institutional administrators, confronting the challenge of getting organized for government grant programs, have a variety of functional models to choose from. But more important than administrative structures is the identification and selection of the government grants administrator.*

Government grants for research and training have a long tradition in American higher education, as well as in the health and hospital fields. But with the developing problems of funding private health and education programs, Federal

---

*Profile of the Federal Grant Administrator, James J. Pallante, Glassboro State College — from doctoral dissertation at Rutgers University, 1974.

Directors of Sponsored Research and Training, Survey by Dr. Perry T. Larsen, University of Utah, Doctoral dissertation, 1974.

Ideas and concepts discussed in Chapter VII are based in part on material from these two recent studies of the Federal Grant Administrator.

grants have become increasingly important and the role of the government grant administrator has been highlighted.

It is only in the last ten years that one finds the concept of a special administrator being discussed and defined. The National Council of University Research Administrators was founded 15 years ago by 30 representatives from a dozen institutions meeting in Washington. At the 1974 annual meeting of NCURA, over 400 research and grant administrators from as many colleges, universities, and leading hospitals were in attendance, and the membership is now over 800.

What do these administrators of sponsored research and training programs do in their jobs? What professional qualifications and characteristics do they have?

In developing his profile of the grant administrator, Dr. Pallante surveyed administrators assigned to "Federal grant administration" whose home institution received combined Federal aid for fiscal year 1970 at or above the national average of $1,358,012.

This survey includes a tabulation of major job responsibilities in order of ascending importance:

1. Identification of Federal (government) programs which might support projects of interest to the faculty.

2. Administration of grants from time of award to time of completion.

3. Communication of information regarding programs to faculty (staff of other institutions).

4. Information of changes in grant policies and procedures.

5. Assistance in the preparation of proposals until completed.

6. Institution-based Federal agency liaison (Washington) for the college/university, etc.

7. Transmitting faculty (staff) interests to the appropriate agencies.

8. Maintaining contacts with other universities, institutions, and related organizations for aid in solving grant-related administration problems.

These are the actual job tasks — related in order of importance by a representative sample of grant administrators. To this list I would add possibly three additional assignments:

1. To be the official representative of the institution as "authorized official" for proposals submitted to outside agencies.

2. To keep an accurate file of current research and training projects; publish an annual report of projects completed or in progress at the institution; publish such other timely publications such as bulletins, etc., to keep the institution informed of the ongoing projects as well as to inform the several communities the institution serves and the public at large.

3. To be the administrator of the funds for institutionally supported research, but with funds disbursed according to policies and decisions from professional staff.

The above three tasks, in my opinion, are essential to the role of the grant administrator who is responsible for the entire grant process within the institution.

Selecting the Chief Administrator

On the basis of the discussion so far, it should be clear to the reader that the position of chief administrator for the Office of Sponsored Programs is both a staff and line or functional position. The staff function involves advising the professional staff and the institutional administrators on policy and procedures for sponsored programs.

The functional responsibilities relate specifically to the assignment to review and approve grant proposals, supervise management of grant budgets and financial reporting on grant projects.

Should the grant administrator be a professional scientist or program administrator? One course of action often considered is to appoint as grant director a faculty or staff person who has had personal grant experience as a project director. In Chapter II, I reported on the practice by grantee institutions of employing former top government agency executives.

Research to date indicates that previous extensive personal grant experience is not a prerequisite for successful grant administration. Appointing a chemist who had experience with NSF grants might not be a wise choice in an institution that has grant capabilities in the social science field, or education, or health, etc. The most important qualification can best be summed up under the term generalist.''

a. Possesses ability to deal tactfully with all administrative and professional personnel in the institution.

b. Has generally a clear understanding of the budget and financial process and both the professional and administrative function of the institution.

c. Is able to understand and keep up to date on government grant programs and policy.

The Pallante study contains an interesting list of qualifications categorized "of *least* importance."

1. Has a record of being a pre-existing faculty or professional staff member.

2. Displays evidence of a publication background.

3. Possesses business background, profit and loss experience.

4. Has had management training in industry.

5. Has an earned doctoral degree.

6. Was previously employed primarily in government agencies.

What does this all tell us?

Some previous experience as a faculty member or scientist is useful; experience in, or special knowledge of Federal government can be important; administrative and management talents are necessary; tactfulness, ability to communicate, good judgment, and broad understanding of administrative and professional concerns are basic.

To conclude this section, is a summary of the grant administrator profile from the Pallante Study.

FEDERAL GRANT ADMINISTRATOR
(General Information Profile)

Holding Position. . . . . 6 years +
Position in existence . . . . 6 years +
Age . . . . 44½ years
Sex . . . . Male
Prior Work Experience. Varied
Academic preparation. . . . . B.A., M.A., Ph.D.
Salary. $20,177
Contract. . . . . 12 month
Working time on grants . . . . 75-100% of time

Academic credits for grants work .... Minimal number
Appointment to position .... From another job within
the college/university
Immediate supervisor........................ Varied
From - Pallante, Profile of the Federal Grant Administrator.

Alternative Institutional Models

There are at least four administrative structural arrangements currently being used by institutions receiving substan-
tial amounts of government grants. These are the Office for
Sponsored Programs, Vice President for Research, Office for
Development and Special Projects, and the Inter-staff Model
which allocates the work to other institutional offices.

The Office for Sponsored Programs

In the Larsen survey of 135 institutions, this was the typical
office structure, most frequently titled Office of Research
Administrator, Sponsored Project Office, or Office of Grants
& Contracts. The functions performed by this unit are the 11
job activities previously outlined in this chapter.

The staffing depends on the scope of government grant
activity. At a minimum there is a director and a secretary.
Additional associates and clerical assistants provide grant
budget development and analysis and expenditure review,
and maintain project files on all grants.

In summary, there are three major functions:

a) assisting the professional staff to identify programs and
sources of funds for sponsored research, training and
service projects;

b) arranging for official authorization of proposals for submission to granting agencies, and assisting in the preparation and processing of such proposals.

c) directing the fiscal administration of all sponsored programs.

Vice President for Research

In research-oriented universities and hospitals, the Vice-President for Research provides central administration supervision for the Office of Sponsored Programs. There is need for policy supervision in allocation of skilled professional resources as between the sponsored research activities of the staff and the other teaching or medical service duties. The final determination as to percent of time and effort of the staff and the rate of reimbursement for work on sponsored projects is a major policy issue.

Development Model

Occasionally, responsibility for government grant development will be assigned to the Development Office. I was recently visited by a colleague from another institution who has the title, "faculty assistant to the development office." He is working half-time with the faculty on government research and training grant proposals.

This is one way to get started, but I mention this approach mainly to caution against it. I believe it can be very confusing to both the staff who must write the proposal, and to the government agencies, if grant applications are a Development Office activity. Development is perceived as promotion, fund-raising-cultivation, public relations. Government grants are perceived as scholarly, academic, scientific, based on merit and entitlement.

The Inter-Staff Model

In a small institution, it may be quite effective to divide grant responsibilities:

1. Assign grant information, proposal review, approval and submission to an academic or scientific staff person.

2. Leave all fiscal management aspects to the financial office, hoping that the two offices will be able to coordinate their work.

None of the above organizational plans will work well if the President of the institution does not play his role as the chief grants officer. Leadership, support, assistance, and sometimes mediation from the top administrator are essential for a vigorous program of government grant support.

NCURA And SRA

National Council of University Research Administrators is the professional organization for sponsored program directors in institutions of higher education.

Society of Research Administrators is a twin organization which includes professional grant administrators from hospitals, private research institutes, and private industry.

Both organizations hold regional and national conferences and workshops in which all aspects of government grant activity are explored, evaluated and discussed.

Cost of membership is nominal and information provided, especially for new administrators, can be very useful.

CHAPTER 8

Grant Information Systems

Accurate, current information about government grant programs, as a basic component of the grant process, was stressed in Chapter I. Here, in specific form is a survey of the most important available government program information sources.

Catalogue of Federal Domestic Assistance
  (to order: write to)

> 1974 Catalogue of Federal Domestic Assistance
> Superintendent of Documents
> Government Printing Office
> Washington, D.C. 20402

The "Catalogue" is a comprehensive listing and description of Federal programs and activities which provide assistance or benefits to the American public. It includes 975 programs administered by 52 different Federal departments, independent agencies, commissions, and councils. The primary purpose of the Catalogue is to aid potential grantees in identifying programs and obtaining information on grants.

It is the best and essential single source of information about Federal grants. It is essential because the grant catalogue number must be included in every grant application. It is the best and primary source because it is so complete.

Being comprehensive and complete, the "Catalogue" appears incomprehensible to some users at first glance. But a careful study and use of the index system makes it easy. All 975 programs are indexed in 4 ways:

1. By *Agency Program,* which lists all programs by Federal Agency sponsor.

2. By *Functional Index,* listing programs by purposes such as education, housing, health, community development, etc.

3. By *Popular Name,* listing programs by such names as Medicare, Title I, ESEA, Higher Education Act of 1965, etc.

4. By a detailed *Subject* Index.

To all seekers after government grants, I urge "Try the Catalogue, you'll like it." A review of the Catalogue page on the Head Start Program shows the completeness of the information provided:

13,600 CHILD DEVELOPMENT-HEAD START
(Head Start)

FEDERAL AGENCY: OFFICE OF THE SECRETARY, DEPARTMENT OF HEALTH, EDUCATION, AND WELFARE.
AUTHORIZATION: 42 U.S.C. 2781 et seq.; Economic Opportunity Act of 1964 as amended; Public Law 91-177, Title II; 81 Stat. 698, as amended by 83 Stat. 828.

OBJECTIVES: To provide educational, nutritional, and social services to preschool children of the poor and their families and involve parents in activities with their children so that the child enters school on equal terms with his less deprived classmates.

TYPES OF ASSISTANCE: Project Grants; Research Contracts.

USES AND USE RESTRICTIONS: 90 percent of the enrollees in a program must come from families whose income is below the poverty guidelines as established. Head Start also sponsors intensive training programs for employees of Child Development Associates.

ELIGIBILITY REQUIREMENTS:

Applicant Eligibility: Any public or private nonprofit agency which meets the requirements may apply for a grant.

Beneficiary Eligibility: Full-year Head Start programs are primarily for children from age 3 up to the age when the child enters the school system, but may include some younger children. Summer Head Start programs are for children who will be attending kindergarten or elementary school for the first time in the fall.

Credentials/Documentation: Forms to certify grantee eligibility may be obtained from the HEW Regional Offices.

APPLICATION AND AWARD PROCESS:

Preapplication Coordination: Grantee submits eligibility documents to the Regional Office or headquarters office 180 days before funding date. The grantee, policy advisory group, and the Head Start community representative participate in a pre-review to develop plans and priorities. The standard applicaton forms as furnished by the Federal agency and required by OMB Circular No. A-102 must be used for this program. Applications should be reviewed under procedures in Part I of OMB Circular No. A-95 (revised).

Application Procedure: The Office of Child Development/Head Start regional representative will provide each applicant agency with a completed check list form showing exactly which items must be completed by each applicant and delegate agency.

Award Procedure: All funds are awarded directly to the grantees. Funds for local Head Start programs, some experimental programs and some career development and technical assistance programs are awarded by the Regional Offices. However, funds for the following are awarded by OCD Headquarters: Indian programs (reservation only); Migrant programs; Parent and Child Center programs; evaluation studies; some experimental programs and some career development training and technical assistance programs. Notification of grant awards must be made to the designated State Central Information Reception Agency and to Department of the Treasury on SF 240.

Deadlines: Eligibility documents are submitted 180 days before the anticipated approval date of the grant. Formal funding request must be received 100 days before approval date.

Range of Approval/Disapproval Time: 150 days from submission of eligibility documents to Governor's approval of grant and release of funds.

Appeals: The HEW Regional Offices and the grantee consider jointly the objectives of the program and the means of achieving these goals.

Renewals: HEW Regional Offices will inform grantees of the application procedures for renewal.

ASSISTANCE CONSIDERATIONS:

Formula and Matching Requirements: 20 percent local share must be supplied. This share may be in cash or in kind: providing space, equipment, utilities or personnel services.

Length and Time Phasing of Assistance: Summer Head Start — Minimum 120 hours. Full-year Head Start—full day or part day but minimum of 3 hours per day in an 8- to 12-month period.

POST ASSISTANCE REQUIREMENTS:

Reports: Quarterly financial and program progress reports are required. Statement of estimated unexpended funds is due 90 days after end of the program year.

Audits: All grantees must arrange for an annual audit due 120 days after the end of the year. Preliminary audit surveys are mandatory for grantees who have not been audited according to Head Start requirements in the past 12 months.

Records: Grantee must maintain an accounting system adequate to meet the purposes of the grant. A statement signed by the appropriate public financial officer or licensed public accountant must be submitted with the initial grant.

FINANCIAL INFORMATION:

Account Identification: 09-80-0136-0-1-999.

Obligations: (Grants) FY 73 $392,100,000; FY 74 $392,100,000; and FY 75 est $430,000,000.

Range and Average of Financial Assistance: $1,500 to $12,000,000; (Estimate of average is not applicable).

PROGRAM ACCOMPLISHMENTS: Since 1965, Head Start has served 4,941,500 children from low-income families in 50 states, Puerto Rico, the Virgin Islands, and the Pacific Trust Territories. The program has improved the quality of life for these children by providing educational experiences, improving their health, assuring that they receive proper nutrition, and providing social and psychological help to them and their families. During fiscal year 1973, Head Start served 379,000 children in full-year, summer, and experimental programs. During fiscal 1972, Head Start launched the following limited pilot programs: Health Start in 29 localities; Home Start in 16 localities; child advocacy components in seven existing Parent and Child Centers. In fiscal year 1973 the Child and Family Resource Program (11 sites) was added.

REGULATIONS, GUIDELINES, AND LITERATURE: "Head Start Manual of Policies and Instructions," no charge; "Head Start: A Child Development Program," no charge.

INFORMATION CONTACTS:

Regional or Local Office: Regional Program Director, Office of Child Development, Office of Human Development, HEW Regional Offices (see appendix for listing).

Headquarters Office: Office of Child Development/Head Start, Office of Human Development, Department of Health, Education, and Welfare, P.O. Box 1182, Washington, DC 20013. Telephone: (202) 755-7790.

RELATED PROGRAMS: 13.601, Child Development-Technical Assistance; 13.443, Follow Through; 13.444, Handicapped Early Childhood Assistance; 13.511, Educationally Deprived Children-Special Grants for Urban and Rural Schools; 13.512, Educationally Deprived Children-Special Incentive Grants: 13.707, Child Welfare Services.

Federal Register

(The Federal Register will be furnished by mail to subscribers, free of postage, for $5.00 per month or $45 per year, payable in advance. Remit checks or money order, made payable to the Superintendent of Documents, U.S. Government Printing Office, Washington, D.C. 20402.)

Published 2 or 3 days each week, the Register is the *official* source of *guidelines* and *regulations* for all U.S. government programs, including grant programs. It is also the official publication source for deadlines for submitting grant proposals.

Probably less than 10% of the information included in the Register would have any application to the interests of a particular health, education or social service institution. But a regular review of the Register will provide first knowledge about new regulations or changes in old programs. It will serve as a warning signal for deadlines for grant applications.

Finally, some major Federal agencies, such as the U.S. Office of Education, now limit all regular agency wide publication on their grant programs — to the Federal Register.

The *Highlights* on the cover page for the Nov. 20, 1974 issue is illustrative of the kind of information available.

Supplementing the "Catalogue" and the "Register," which provide government-wide program information, are the infor-

WEDNESDAY, NOVEMBER 20, 1974

WASHINGTON, D.C.

Volume 39 ■ Number 225

Pages 40739–40846

HIGHLIGHTS OF THIS ISSUE

This listing does not affect the legal status
of any document published in this issue. Detailed
table of contents appears inside.

(Continued inside)

mation sources and publications from individual Federal agencies.

National Science Foundation

N.S.F. provides by far the most informative and useful program information materials of any Federal agency. With an annual budget of over $600 million and 58 programs — the foundation has individual program announcements available for each grant activity.

1. *Guide to Programs, National Science Foundation*
   The guide provides summary information about all assistance programs. Individual program listings include basic program information, closing dates and the address from which more detailed information, brochures, and application forms may be obtained.

2. *N.S.F. Organizational Directory*
   Names, N.S.F. Office Room number, and telephone numbers for all N.S.F. program staff listed by program areas, are provided.

3. *Grants for Scientific Research*
   Manual containing all necessary information for preparing an application for a research grant. This is the best publication available anywhere on preparation of a research grant proposal.

4. *N.S.F. Data Book*
   Provides a wide variety of useful facts about allocation of N.S.F. grants by areas of science — by states, by size of grants, etc. — including a table on "average distribution

of funds by type of expenditure — for scientific research projects," i.e., an actual average (typical) grant budget.

5. *Guides for Preparation of Proposals*
Copies are available for most all N.S.F. individual programs — as listed in the "Guide to Programs."

6. *Bulletin*
Published monthly — the bulletin includes program deadlines for upcoming proposals. All of the above publications are available from the
National Science Foundation
1800 G Street, N.W.
Washington, D.C. 20550
Attn: Central Processing Section.
There is no charge for single copies.

National Endowment for the Humanities

1. *National Endowment for the Humanities*
Program Announcements 1974-75
Information provided includes general information for all applications, calendar of application deadlines, and specific program information for Division of Research Grants, Fellowships, Education Programs, Public Programs, Youth grants; and a staff directory.

2. *Education Programs*
Included is program information and guidelines for the Education section of the Endowment.
(Above publication may be ordered from
National Endowment for the Humanities
806 15th St., N.W.
Washington, D.C. 20506).

National Endowment for the Arts

1. *New Dimensions for the Arts*
   Descriptions of all program activities for the NEA are provided, as well as a complete listing of the previous year's grants.

2. *National Endowment for the Arts*
   What It Is, What It Does
   Capsule program and project information is provided and general grant application information.
   (Copies of these publications available from:
   Program Information
   National Endowment for the Arts
   806 15th St., N.W.
   Washington, D.C. 20530).

Law Enforcement Assistance Administration

LEAA Newsletter
Published 10 times a year, the Newsletter provides program grant information and announcements of grant awards. LEAA program priorities are listed. Available from:
   LEAA Newsletter
   Public Information Office
   Law Enforcement Assistance Adm.
   U.S. Dep't. of Justice
   Washington, D.C. 20530

Grant Administration Publications

The following publications provide detailed information on

the procedure for operation and management of government grants from the agencies as indicated. Single copies are available free of charge.

1. *National Science Foundation, Grant Administration Manual* (order from N.S.F., Washington D.C. 20550)__

2. *Related DHEW, and N.I.H. manuals*
   a. *DHEW Grants Administration manual* ((Available from the Superintendent of Documents, U.S. Government Printing Office, Washington D.C. 20402.)
   b. *A Guide to Grant and Award Programs of the National Institutes of Health.* PHS Publication No. 1067.
   c. *Application Forms and Instructions.*
   d. *Special Information and Instructions on NIH Support of Meetings.*
   e. *NIH-DRG Newsletter.* Published monthly by the Division of Research Grants, NIH, and provided to grantee institutions.
   f. *NIH Guide for Grants and Contracts.* Published at irregular intervals by the NIH to provide new and revised policy, program, and administrative information on NIH's grant and contract programs. Provided to grantee institutions.
   (Copies of the above documents are generally available in administrative offices of the grantee institution. Additional copies usually may be obtained from the Division of Research Grants, NIH, Bethesda, Maryland 20014, except as noted for the DHEW Grants Administration Manual.)

A concluding note is in order about commercial grant information sources. Almost every month a new commercial service on government program information is announced. They range in cost from $50 to $600 per year. The best known series is the Commerce Clearing House Report.

This writer has subscribed to several of the different services, and I have concluded that the government agencies' own reports are the most useful. If the institution's Office for Sponsored Programs can assign a staff person almost full time to receive and index and follow up with research from the commercial services, they can be worthwhile.

Finally, the securing, analysis, and distribution of current, pertinent information about government grants to the professional staff of your institution can be one of the most powerful motivational factors for getting grants.

CHAPTER 9

Getting a Grant — Three Case Studies

Up to now, we have tried to make clear both theory and practice involved in the securing of government grants. Both theory and practice will become still more sharply defined in the following case examples of Federal grants obtained by Fordham University. As the reader will note, the grants were for vastly different purposes. In each instance, we are giving a "blow by blow" accounting with the actual dates, discussions, and correspondence included.

CASE STUDY ONE

Project Title: Social Work for Drug Abuse;
Training Grant, National Institute of Mental Health—
MH 13209-01

December, 1971

James R. Dumpson, Dean of the School of Social Service, reported on several occasions — in discussions with the Director of Research Services — on plans for a major training grant application to the National Institute of Mental Health to strengthen faculty capabilities and train Masters degree social workers to address the serious drug abuse situation in the South Bronx.

Three factors made such an application practical at this time.

1. The National Institute of Mental Health, Division of Narcotic Addiction Drug Abuse, had earmarked funds for drug abuse projects. New York City was a target area.

2. The School of Social Service had employed a new faculty member, Maria M. Correa, who had long experience working in the South Bronx as a public health consultant and was available to direct a new training program to combat drug abuse which was spreading widely in the area.

3. Jose H. Vazquez, Director of a South Bronx drug abuse agency, was seeking help from Fordham School of Social Service.

January 20, 1972:

Mr. Vazquez, by letter, advised Dean Dumpson that he found the Fordham proposal, which he had reviewed, "very realistic, and await commencement of operations in July."

The proposed training grant would provide for establishment of a Practice and Teaching Center to be jointly operated by Fordham University School of Social Service and the South Bronx Model Cities Drug Abuse Program.

Mr. Vazquez' letter and his professional resume were attached to the training grant application.

This constituted evidence of official community endorsement and support to permit Fordham faculty and students to work with the patients and clients in the South Bronx.

February 8, 1972:

Training Grant application submitted to the National

Institute of Mental Health.

Funds were requested to support 3 faculty, 2 secretaries, and 15 Masters degree trainees. $133,612 was requested for the first year to begin 9/1/72 and for 4 additional years for a total of $778,901.

February 23, 1972:

Rep. Herman Badillo, member of Congress, 21st District, New York (includes the South Bronx) wrote to Dr. Vernon E. Wilson, Administrator, Health Services and Mental Health Administration.

"I am pleased to have this opportunity to express my deep interest in and strong support of the recently submitted proposal of the Fordham University School of Social Service for a graduate training program in social work and drug abuse.

"Fordham proposes the establishment of a Drug Addiction Practice and Teaching Center in conjunction with a drug addiction program conducted by the South Bronx Model Cities Program. Professor Maria M. Correa, the program director, envisions that the Center will give essential exposure to 15 graduate students to a comprehensive drug addiction program which is fighting drug use and abuse among Puerto Ricans who reside in the *barrio* of the South Bronx. It is anticipated that the traineeships would be awarded to Puerto Rican students from economically deprived backgrounds.

"I have reviewed this proposal and believe it has a great potential for not only providing a valuable educational experience but also in terms of grappling with one of the most critical issues affecting a large segment of my constituency in the South Bronx. I am intimately aware of the drug abuse problem in this area of my district and, as a faculty member of Fordham, I also realize the great service this program will be doing to the students.

"I am wholeheartedly in support of this program and urge that you and other appropriate officials give Fordham's proposal your fullest, most careful and sympathetic consideration with a view toward expediting its processing and recommending it for approval.

"I will appreciate being kept informed of developments on this matter and would be glad to discuss the problem with you and your staff.

"Sincerely,

"Herman Badillo
"Member of Congress"

The idea of sending this letter had been agreed upon by Dean Dumpson and the Director of Research Services. It was unusual to request a Congressional endorsement for an NIMH training grant, but this was an unusual grant application. It was confronting a problem with which the Congressman himself was deeply and personally familiar.

March 2, 1972:

Memorandum was received from National Institutes of Health acknowledging receipt of grant application and assignment of grant number and date of Council final review, June 1972.

TO   : Financial Officer   DATE: March 2, 1972

           Career Development Review Branch
FROM   : Division of Research Grants
           National Institutes of Health
SUBJECT: Distribution of Training Grant Applications

The attached copies of a recently submitted application for Public Health Service support are enclosed for distribution in accordance with institutional requirements.

The action taken on this application will be sent as soon as possible after advisory council review. The month in which the council will meet is shown in the upper right-hand corner of the first page of the application. Any correspondence regarding this application should indicate the reference number that has been assigned.

Your cooperation in handling the distribution within your institution is greatly appreciated.

May 19, 1972:
Dean Dumpson was advised by phone, by NIMH, on May 19, that it would be necessary to revise and expand the proposal submitted by Fordham. The deadline for considering the revised proposal for submission for final approval at the June NIMH Council meeting was May 30.
Revisions and additions suggested by NIMH:
1) Add research personnel to staff to provide for development of research skills for trainees and ongoing research and evaluation of the project.

2) Provide course outlines for all the new courses and seminars to be developed, including complete bibliographies.

3) Explain how the regular social work curriculum was to be adapted for the drug abuse training project.

The first year budget request was increased from $133,612 to $178,412.

May 22, 1972:
Rep. Herman Badillo wrote a letter to Dr. Jerome H. Jaffe, Special Consultant to the President for Narcotics and Dangerous Drugs.
Repeating the endorsement of the project as contained

in his earlier letter to Dr. Wilson of NIMH, Badillo's letter concluded:

"It is imperative that this program be implemented as soon as possible, and this is my reason for appealing to you. A site visit has been made, and Fordham is furnishing additional information which was requested. However, with the length of review procedure and a reported restriction in funds, it may not be implemented until sometime in the late fall, thus creating virtually insurmountable problems for the school and students. I urge, therefore, that you and other appropriate officials take whatever steps may be necessary to expedite and approve this outstanding proposal."

May 24, 1972:

The amended application was prepared and delivered by a faculty member to NIMH in Bethesda, Maryland.

July 6, 1972:

Memorandum advising that revised application had been received by NIMH was received by Fordham.

July 15, 1972:

Notice of Grant Award received by Fordham University from NIMH.

Note the following:

Starting date for project July 1, 1972.

Total grant award 1st year $110,371 (there was a cutback in trainees support from 15 to 8.)

Support was recommended for 4 additional years.

DEPARTMENT OF HEALTH, EDUCATION, AND WELFARE

Public Health Service

NOTICE OF GRANT AWARDED

Under Authority of Federal Statutes and Regulations, and Public
Health Service Policy Statements applicable to:

[ ] Research Grant   [X] Training Grant

[ ]

DT

DATE ISSUED:	
Grant Number	
1 T31 MH13209-01	**MHST**
TOTAL PROJECT PERIOD:	
From **07/01/72** Through **06/30/77**	
GRANT PERIOD:	
From **07/01/72** Through **06/30/77**	

e of Project or Area of Training **SOCIAL WORK - DRUG ABUSE**

Grantee Institution	Principal Investigator or Program Director
FORDHAM UNIVERSITY **BRONX, N Y 10458** 24	**CORREA, MARIA M** **MD** **FORDHAM UNIV SCHOOL OF SOC SER** **LINCOLN CENTER** **NEW YORK, N Y 10023**

APPROVED BUDGET		AWARD COMPUTATION	
R BUDGET PERIOD **07/01/72** Through **06/30/73**		1. DIRECT COSTS .... $	**103,476**
rsonnel .... $ 60,310		2. INDIRECT COSTS .... $	**6,895**
nsultant Services* 2,400		(Calculated at _____ rate)	
uipment*		TOTAL .... $	**110,371**
pplies 500		4. Less Unobligated Balance from	
vel – Domestic* 450		Prior Budget Period(s) .... $	**0**
vel – Foreign*			
spitalization*			
tpatient Costs*			
erations and Renovations*		5. AMOUNT OF THIS AWARD ———→ $	**110,371**
plication Costs*			
er 2,00		SUPPORT RECOMMENDED FOR REMAINDER OF PROJECT PERIOD	
otal Teaching Costs 85,443		(Subject to the Availability of Funds) Teaching Costs Trainee Cos	
inee Stipends* .....(8 .) .... 19,536[1]/			
inee Tuition and Fees*			
inee Travel*			
otal Trainee Costs 51,757			
TAL DIRECT COSTS ———→ $ 103,476			

Budget Period	Total Direct Costs	Teaching Costs	Trainee Costs
02	**137,200**	85,443	51,757
03	**137,200**	85,443	51,757
04	**169,000**	93,987	75,013
05	**115,500**	72,684	42,816
06	**NONE**		

steriks indicate limited or restricted budget categories

countability for equipment: [ ] conditionally waived [X] not waived

marks **INDIRECT COST ALLOWANCES LIMITED TO 8% OF TOTAL ALLOWABLE DIRECT COSTS**
SUBJECT TO DOWNWARD ADJUSTMENT IF ACTUAL RATE IS LESS.

[1]/ Includes $5,136 dependency allowances.

EM 400533

mon Account Number	PHS Account No.	PHS List Number	PHS Transaction Number
2-3964014 **FY 72**	**733370**	MD-23-72	**01-0H2926**

ments on this grant will be made to:

Recommending National Advisory Council or Committee
MENTAL HEALTH

Signature of PHS Official

CONTROLLER
FORDHAM UNIVERSITY
BRONX, N Y 10458

RICHARD PHILLIPSON, M.D.
DIVISION OF NARCOTIC ADDICTION
AND DRUG ABUSE
NATIONAL INST. OF MENTAL HEALTH

1533
11 69   DISTRIBUTION: [ ] Principal Investigator or Program Director   [ ] Payee   [ ] Public Relations Officer

CASE STUDY TWO

Project Title: John Trumbull (1756-1843): Patriot Artist of the American Revolution (CH-8715)
Research Grant awarded to Fordham University by the National Endowment for the Humanities.

September 15, 1972:

Professor Irma B. Jaffee, came to the Office of Research Services to discuss her research plans and needs. She had just received a contract for publication of a book on the life and works of John Trumbull, the American artist, best known for his famous painting of the signing of the Declaration of Independence.

She had already done 2 years of research but would need at least 2 more years of work to complete the book. Dr. Jaffee, professor of Art History, was planning to apply for a sabbatical leave for the academic year 1973-74. This would provide her with free time and half-salary. She needed additional funds for salary support and research expense.

I suggested she consider an application for a research grant to the National Endowment for the Humanities. I gave her a copy of the page on Humanities Research from the Catalogue of Federal Domestic Programs and suggested we discuss a proposal after she had studied the program requirements. I also gave her the phone number for the N.E.H. program director, Dr. Simone Reagor, and urged her to phone and discuss the research idea informally and directly.

(Catalogue page on N.E.H. Research Grants follows).

45.105 PROMOTION OF THE HUMANITIES-
RESEARCH GRANTS

FEDERAL AGENCY: NATIONAL ENDOWMENT FOR THE HUMANITIES, NATIONAL FOUNDATION ON THE ARTS AND THE HUMANITIES.

AUTHORIZATION: National Foundation on the Arts and Humanities Act of 1965; Public Law 89-209 as amended by Public Law 90-348 and Public Law 91-346; 20 U.S.C. 951-3.

OBJECTIVES: To fund, wholly or partially, research projects which contribute to knowledge and understanding of the humanities.

TYPES OF ASSISTANCE: Project Grants.

USES AND USE RESTRICTIONS: Grants support the basic costs of research and editing projects, usually collaborative, including travel, per diem payments, supplies and appropriate research assistance. Payment for purchases of equipment is not allowable nor is payment for released time for academic persons. Full support for an individual scholar's research is automatically considered by NEH Division of fellowships and stipends.

ELIGIBILITY REQUIREMENTS:

Applicant Eligibility: U.S. citizens and residents in U.S. territories and U.S. learned societies, organizations, and academic institutions (or their employees whether or not they are citizens) are eligible. Foreign institutions or organizations are not eligible and foreign nationals are also ineligible unless affiliated with a U.S. institution or organization.

Beneficiary Eligibility: Same as applicant eligibility.

Credentials/Documentation: None

APPLICATION AND AWARD PROCESS:

Preapplication Coordination: Draft proposals should be reviewed by staff prior to formal application.

Application Procedure: Direct application to Division of Research Grants, National Endowment for the Humanities. Application instructions provided by the Division upon receipt of eligible draft proposal.

Award Procedure: Applications are reviewed by experts in the subject area and panels of scholars and other appropriate individuals. Awards are made by the Chairman of the National Endowment for the Humanities after recommendation by the National Council on the Humanities.

Deadlines: Twice a year, in spring and in the fall. Write to Division Director, address below, for specific information.

Range of Approval/Disapproval Time: About 8 months.

Appeals: None.

Renewals: Renewal grants are made and are processed as new applications.

ASSISTANCE CONSIDERATIONS:

Formula and Matching Requirements: Cost sharing is generally required at about 10 percent.

Length and Time Phasing of Assistance: Up to 36 months.

POST ASSISTANCE REQUIREMENTS:

Reports: Final narrative report 3 months after termination of grant; short progress reports with each request for payment.

Audits: Final audits may be made at the direction of the Chairman of the Endowment for up to 3 years after termination of grant.

Records: Any and all records and journals required for audit under generally accepted accounting systems.

FINANCIAL INFORMATION:

Account Identification: 31-35-0100-0-1-605.

Obligations: (Grants) FY 73 $4,408,540; FY 75 est. $3,290,000; and FY 75 est $4,000,000.

Range and Average of Financial Assistance: $2,500 to $300,000; $25,000.

PROGRAM ACCOMPLISHMENTS: During fiscal year 1973, grants awarded for research projects totaled 222.

REGULATIONS, GUIDELINES, AND LITERATURE: 45 CFR 1100 and 1105. National Endowment for the Humanities, Eighth Annual Report (fiscal year 1973). Available from Superintendent of Documents, U.S. Government Printing Office, Washington, DC 20402. National Endowment for the Humanities, Program Information for Applicants 1973-74, available on request from National Endowment for the Humanaties, Washington, DC 20506.

INFORMATION CONTACTS:

Regional or Local Office: None.

Headquarters Office: Director, Division of Research Grants, National Endowment for the Humanities, Washington, DC 20506. Telephone: (202) 382-5857.

RELATED PROGRAMS: 45.104, Promotion of the Humanities-Media Grants.

September 22, 1972:

Dr. Jaffee advised me that she had talked with the National Endowment; they said that her research plan was of interest to them and had sent her an application form, which she had with her.

We studied the program guidelines and noted several technical details.

November 15, 1972 was the next deadline for submitting applications. She could meet that.

N.E.H. expected the grantee institution to "cost-share" at least 10% of the total cost of the project. Dr. Jaffe's ½ salary for the sabbatical year would more than cover that requirement.

$25,000 was the average N.E.H. grant amount. Her budget estimate was $24,000.

We agreed that she would go ahead to write up the proposal for a grant beginning on July 1, 1973.

November 9, 1972:

The Research Grant Application for the Trumbull project was reviewed by the Director of Research Services and signed on behalf of the University.

November 20, 1972:

Dr. Simone Reagor, Assistant Director, Division of Research Grants, N.E.H., advised Dr. Jaffee by letter (with copy to Director of Research Services at Fordham) that N.E.H. had received the grant application. It had been assigned application #H-8715.

The letter went on to say that the application was receiving staff review for conformity to technical requirements; that it would be submitted to a panel of established scholars in the field for opinions and recommendations; that it would subsequently be reviewed by a panel of humanists and acted upon by the Chairman, and the National Council in May, 1973.

June 12, 1973

Mr. Neil Big, program specialist, Division of Research Grants, N.E.H., phoned to advise the Director of Research Services at Fordham that the Trumbull project had been approved for funding, but at a maximum level of $20,000 (rather than $24,000).

I agreed to phone him back with some suggested budget adjustments.

Dr. Jaffe by phone from her home agreed to the budget cuts, specifically a cutback on technical consultants from $5000 to $2000, which would result in a reduction of the indirect cost allowance from $5 to $3000 — thus reducing the whole budget to $19,141 — for the grant from N.E.H.

The adjusted budget was put into the mail to Mr. Big — countersigned by Dr. Jaffe and the Director of Research Services.

June 26, 1973:

The grant award letter was received at Fordham University. It follows:

Mr. Philip H. DesMarais   JUN 2 6 1973
Director
Research Services
Fordham University
Bronx, New York 10458

Dear Mr. DesMarais:

It is a pleasure to inform you that, in accordance with the application identified as H-8715 and Professor Jaffe's letters of June 13, 1973, a grant of $19,141 is awarded to Fordham University in support of the project entitled "John Trumbull (1756-1843): Patriot Artist of The American Revolution" under the direction of Professor Irma B. Jaffe.

"General Grant Provisions," dated July 1, 1972, are applicable to this award and are enclosed. The revised budget submitted on June 13, 1973, is approved as the official program against which grant expenditures may be lodged, and the following specific provisions will be applicable to this award:

1. Allowable costs shall be determined in accordance with the cost principles set forth in the Office of Management and Budget Circular A-21, as amended to date.

2. Institutional cost sharing shall not be less than the $10,400 shown in the budget.

3. The indirect cost rate of 24% of salaries and wages is accepted as a fixed, predetermined rate for the duration of this award.

The identifying number for this grant is RB-8715-73-450 and the grant period is July 1, 1973 through August 31, 1974. Commitment of grant funds can be made during this period only, and must be for materials and services used during this same period.

Endowment reporting requirements are described in Enclosures 1 and 2. For this grant, interim expenditures reports must be submitted quarterly throughout the grant period with the first report due as of September 30, 1973. Payments will be made upon request as described in Enclosure 1 and in Section 4 of the "Provisions." All reports, payment requests, and correspondence pertaining to this award should be addressed to our Division of Research Grants.

Please confirm acceptance of this grant and the conditions attached to it by signing the copy of this letter and returning it in the enclosed envelope.

We look forward to the significant contribution this project will make to the humanities. If any questions arise in regard to it, or if the Endowment can be of assistance as the project proceeds, please feel free to contact the Division of Research Grants.

Sincerely yours,

Ronald Berman
Chairman

Enclosures

cc: Professor Irma B. Jaffe
Mr. James M. Kenny

June 29, 1973:

The letter of acceptance of the grant was mailed to the Director, National Endowment for the Humanities, and it follows:

Dr. Ronald Berman
Chairman
National Endowment for the Humanities
Washington, D.C. 20506

Dear Dr. Berman:

Thank you very much for your letter of June 26, 1973, announcing the award to Fordham University of a research grant for Professor Irma Jaffe. Her project is entitled, "John Trumbull (1756-1843): Patriot Artist of The American Revolution."

Fordham is most grateful for the support received from the Endowment for this research. You and your colleagues are to be congratulated for the excellent efforts you are making to develop the program of the Endowment to that it will provide the most comprehensive support possible for education and research in the humanities throughout the United States.

Sincerely yours,

Philip H. Des Marais
Director

What were the important factors involved in the award of the research grant for the Trumbull study by Professor Irma Jaffe?

I believe the most important factor was the professional competence, evidence of research capability, and previous record of publication demonstrated by the principal investigator. By way of illustration, here is the first page of a four-page curriculum vitae for Dr. Jaffe — as included in the proposal.

Education
B.S., *Magna Cum Laude,* Columbia University School of General Studies, 1958.
M.A., Columbia University, Department of Art History and Archaeology, 1960.
Ph.D., Columbia University, Department of Art History and Archaeology, 1966.

Honors
Phi Beta Kappa.
Outstanding Achievement Award. Columbia University School of General Studies, 1958.
Distinguished Alumni Award, Columbia University School of General Studies, 1965.

Positions
Docent, Whitney Museum of American Art, 1963-64.
Research Curator, Whitney Museum of American Art, 1964-65.
Adjunct Instructor of Art History, Upsala College (East Orange, N.J.) 1965-66.
Assistant Professor of Art History, Fordham University, 1966-68.
Associate Professor of Art History, Fordham University, 1968-72.
Professor of Art History, Fordham University, 1972—present.

Publications
Books
1. Jaffe, Irma B., *Joseph Stella,* Harvard University Press, 1970.
2. Wittkower, Rudolf, and Jaffe, Irma B. (eds.), *Baroque Art: The Jesuit Contribution.* New York: Fordham University Press, 1972.
3. Baur, John I.H., *Joseph Stella,* Research, Bibliography and Chronology by Irma B. Jaffe, New York: Praeger, 1971.
4. Jaffe, Irma B., "The Forming of the Avant-Garde: 1900-1930," *The Genius of American Painting,* John Wilmerding (ed.), London, Weidenfeld and Nicolson, 1973 (projected publication date). This is a

22,000 word essay with seventy-seven illustrations and full documentation, my contribution to an in-depth survey history of American art.

Articles (Selected List)

1. Jaffe, Irma B. "The Declaration of Independence: Keys and Dates," *American Art Journal*, Fall 1971, pp. 41-49.
2. Jaffe, Irma B. "Fordham's Trumbull Drawings: The Declaration of Independence and Other Discoveries," *American Art Journal*, Spring 1971, pp. 5-38.
3. Jaffe, Irma B. "Antonino Occello and the Castle Chapel at Monesiglio," *Arte Lombarda*, Fall 1971 (Italian translation by G. Colombardo), pp. 243-258.
4. Jaffe, Irma B. "Controversy," *American Scholar*, Spring 1971.
5. Jaffe, Irma B. "A Conversation with Hans Hofmann," *Art Forum*, January 1971, pp. 34-37. Reprinted in *Modern Culture and the Arts*, New York, McGraw Hill, 1972.

CASE STUDY THREE

Project Title: The Human Ecology of Nomadism

Research Grant awarded to Fordham University by the National Science Foundation.

August, 1972:

Professor Warren W. Swidler, Liberal Arts College, Lincoln Center, was in contact with the Office of Research Services on several occasions during the summer of 1972 to discuss possibilities of submitting a research grant application to the National Science Foundation. He outlined circumstances and developments in connection with his research interests that he believed made a good case for getting a grant.

1. He had received a faculty fellowship from the University — for $8000 — to launch his project-research on the life-styles of the nomadic peoples in Pakistan.

2. Preliminary studies in the Baluchistan area of Pakistan had been undertaken by Prof. Swidler for his doctoral thesis at Columbia. His mentors at Columbia, Dr. Margaret Mead, and Dr. Frederick Barth, and he himself were in reality among the few people in the world knowledgeable about the relatively remote and unstudied area. They would strongly support any research proposals he would make.

3. Swidler already had a request for support for the project at the American Council of Learned Societies. It was likely to be funded, but additional funds were needed. It would be at least a three-year project, and ACLS grants were limited to $10-12,000.

September 12, 1972:

Research proposal submitted to the National Science Foundation requesting $14,773 for support of 9 months' research in West Pakistan. The budget request indicated that the University was "cost sharing" $8500 for the project.

Justification for the research emphasized that studies of the pattern of economic activity of the nomadic herding tribes might provide information and insights applicable to preserving the natural environments and resources of advanced countries.

September 18, 1972:

The National Science Foundation acknowledged receipt of the grant proposal and assigned an official proposal number.

October, 1972:

Dr. Swidler, postponing his departure for Pakistan until January, visited the Library of Congress and a Scholar at Duke University, knowledgeable about his area, to have background discussion and contacts.

January 15, 1973:

Letter of grant award received by Fordham University.

NATIONAL SCIENCE FOUNDATION
WASHINGTON, D.C. 20550

JAN 1 5 1973

The Very Reverend James C. Finlay, S.J.,
  President
Fordham University   Grant GS-36891
Bronx, New York 10458   Proposal No. P3S0263

Dear Father Finlay:

It is a pleasure to inform you that $14,600 is granted to
Fordham University for support of the project entitled "The
Human Ecology of Nomadism" as outlined in the above-numbered
proposal. This project is under the direction of Warren W.
Swidler, Department of Social Sciences.

The funds provided by this grant are intended to support the
project for nine months in accordance with the attached budget summary. The grant is effective January 15, 1973 and
will expire on March 31, 1974.

The provisions of Enclosure R-12 are applicable to this grant.

Sincerely yours,

Wilbur W. Bolton, Jr.
Grants Officer

Enclosures

138

April 25, 1973:

Dr. Swidler, by mail from Pakistan, submitted a progress report on the launching of his field research. Included was a request for a renewal of his NSF grant with additional funds totaling $22,000. The renewal period was proposed for October 15, 1973 to October 14, 1974.

The renewal application reported the grant of $10,000 from the American Council of Learned Societies for the period Sept. 15, 1973 to August 31, 1974. This was to conduct research on the effects of irrigation technology on newly settled nomadic communities — a "continuation of one aspect of the present work."

May 25, 1973:

Grant renewal proposal submitted to National Science Foundation.

F O R D H A M   U N I V E R S I T Y   Bronx, N.Y. 10458

May 25, 1973

Dr. John Cornell
Program Director for Anthropology
Division of Social Sciences
National Science Foundation
Washington, D. C. 20550

Dear Dr. Cornell:

Attached please find 20 copies of the proposal from Fordham University for Professor
Warren W. Swidler for renewal request (GS-36891).

If you have any questions regarding this
proposal, please call me at 933-2233, Ext. 572.
Since Dr. Swidler is currently doing field research in Pakistan, my office must handle any
technical matters connected with this proposal.

Sincerely yours,

Philip H. Des Marais
Director

PHD:rs
Encs.

cc: Dr. Warren Swidler
     Dr. Eva Sandis

May 30, 1973:

NSF acknowledged receipt of renewal budget request.

October 1, 1973:

Renewal research grant budget award received by the University.

In view of the support also provided by the ACLS, the renewal budget expanded the total NSF award to $34,800 and extended the grant period for the total project to January 31, 1975.

Case Study Comments

What practical lessons are to be learned from reflecting upon the three grant case studies previously reviewed?

The Drug Abuse training grant suggests (case #1) the following factors:

1. The granting agency had announced funds *earmarked* by the U.S. Congress for prevention and treatment of drug abuse.

2. There was an obvious community need for the professional personnel to be trained.

3. The project was aimed at one of the areas of greatest social and economic distress in the nation. It would have indeed been difficult to reject a proposal to train minority professional personnel to combat drug abuse among minority people in the South Bronx. The University was responding to an urgently felt local community need for which there was national concern.

In the case of the Trumbull study, several proposal aspects seem important.

1. The proposed project director was a mature scholar with prestigious accomplishment in the field of study.

2. The project would produce a handsomely illustrated volume on American historical painting for publication in 1976.

Projects relevant to the Bicentennial were an announced priority for the granting agency.

3. I believe that a woman project director was an appealing factor, at a time when equal opportunity for women scholars is a mandated objective of the Federal government.

The anthropology project involves other helpful factors in successful research grant proposals.

1. The project director was the unique possessor of knowledge about and access to the research subject and area.

2. His major doctoral advisors were scholars of international reputation who could support the application with scholarly authority.

3. The project was being assisted from additional sources, i.e., the University and the American Council of Learned Societies. Thus, for a total investment of $34,000, NSF would get a $50,000 project of absolutely original research with significant implication for problems of world concern — ecology, economic development of emerging third-world peoples, and access to hard-to-get information from one of the most remote areas on the globe.

To sum it all up:

1. Propose to train personnel to attack an urgent local social problem with national implications;

2. Propose project directors with evident high scholarly and scientific attainments — with graduate degrees from prestigious universities, with connections, with endorsements from scholars of international reputation;

3. Propose a research topic which has never been studied before (this should be obvious from the internal evidence of the proposal itself), where there are only two or three other qualified scholars able to evaluate the proposal.

If you can design training or research grant applications with the above criteria, you will probably get the grant.

CHAPTER 10

Model for Policies and Procedures/Government Grant Programs

By way of a final review, I am including this last chapter to serve as a model for policies and procedures for government grant programs.

Statement of Purpose

1.When research and training programs sponsored by individuals or organizations outside the institution require the participation of the institution as party to a contract or as administrator of granted funds, the institution will agree to such participation within the limitation of its physical and financial capacities, if the purpose of the programs coincides with the aims of the institution. Inasmuch as the institution scrupulously avoids any regular institutional judgment as to the choice or validity of subjects for or methods of investigation, this determination will be made by referring to standards of normal academic procedure in each field of inquiry as described by the staff. The opportunity for the institution and the staff to respond to current urgent community problems is provided by participation in sponsored training programs and technical assistance and evaluation services relevant to the objectives of the institution.

2. General Administration

Institution approval and administration of sponsored grant programs is centered in the Office of Sponsored Programs. Under policies formulated by the Trustees and approved by the President of the institution, the Director of Sponsored Programs is responsible for the following functions:

a. The review and approval on behalf of the institution of all proposals and budgets for sponsored research, demonstration and training grant programs prior to submission to the granting agency. This review and approval shall include project requirements for space and other items included in indirect costs. Proposals shall also be reviewed with respect to their compliance with the provisions of Section 4 below, including a specification as to how salaries are related to regular faculty responsibilities.

b. The review and verification of purchase orders under grants.

c. The review and verification of other requests for disbursement of grant funds.

d. The submission of final reports on grants. The Office of Vice-President for Financial Affairs has the responsibility as official custodian of grant funds to establish and maintain grant accounts, set up grant payrolls, and disburse all payments when approved by the budget administrator of the funds and the Director of Sponsored Programs.

3. Procedures for Project Directors

a. Staff members have primary responsibility for preparation of grant proposals. Completed proposals, including necessary endorsements by department chairmen or supervisors should be forwarded to the Office of Sponsored Programs for institution approval. *One week before mailing deadlines should be allowed for this purpose.* One copy for signature and one additional copy for the Office of Sponsored Programs' permanent file should be provided.

b. **Operating Project Budgets**
When the grant award has been received, the project director will be responsible for preparing an operation budget consistent with the grant budget on a form to be supplied by the Office of Sponsored Programs. The Grant Accounts Officer is available to assist in filling out the budget form.
The Office of Sponsored Programs is responsible for supplying copies of project budgets and grant awards to the Financial Office, which will establish an account for each project. A monthly expenditure report is sent to the project directors to inform them of the status of the project budget.

c. **Disbursements**
Purchase orders and other requests for disbursement made by project directors will be sent to the Office of

Sponsored Programs for verification for payment by the Financial Office and the Purchasing Office.

d. **Payrolls**

Project directors will be responsible for determining stipend schedules and payrolls, based on the approved grant operating budget. The payroll office will pay salaries and stipends as authorized by project directors and the Office of Sponsored Programs. Project directors must prepare payroll card and W-4 Form (Withholding Form) for each person paid on the grant budget. These are sent to the Office of Sponsored Programs and forwarded to the Finance Office.

e. **Financial Reports**

The Grants Accounts Officer in the Office of Sponsored Programs prepares interim and final financial reports on sponsored projects.

f. **Responsibilities of Project Directors**

Preparation of interim and final technical reports on sponsored projects is the responsibility of the project director. Monitoring of monthly expenditure reports and checking of expenditure requests against report balances for sufficient funds is also a function of the project director. Any discrepancies should be reported to the Grants Accounts Offices.

4. Guidelines for Fiscal Aspects of Grants

a. **Staff Compensation**

Grant-contract funds may be used to supply part of the base compensation of staff in exchange for a reduction of the normal work load (and concomitant reduction of the institution's contribution to the staff members' compensation). Determination of the amount of reduction and of the responsibilities from which the faculty member will be released is to be agreed to by the staff member involved, the project director, department chairman and appropriate supervisor.

b. **Supplementation for Grant/Contract Efforts**

In direct parallel with opportunities for staff income supplementation in outside activities such as consulting, professional practice, and part-time teaching which do not impair the performance of regular staff duties, the institution does permit supplementation for grant/contract efforts within the institution.

c. **Fringe Benefits**

Staff employed on sponsored projects will be eligible for fringe benefits to the extent that the full costs of these benefits are covered either by the indirect cost allowance or a direct cost element of the grant budget. Current cost tables on fringe benefits as developed by the institution Personnel Office are on file in the Office of Sponsored Programs.

d. **Advance Funding of Grant Programs**

No institution funds will be disbursed unless the institution has a signed contract or, at minimum, a letter of intent from an authorized official of a granting agency. An approved budget must also be on file in the Office of Sponsored Programs. These agreements should clearly spell out the financial terms attending the projects in question and there should be a revolving fund of at least 10% for the project in the institution's Finance Office. In those instances where a revolving fund arrangement cannot be worked out, a schedule of payments from the agency to the institution should be clearly established in advance of any disbursement of institution funds. In those cases where the institution is obliged to make advance payments and otherwise provide the project its working capital, the institution should receive specific reimbursement for this service as included in the indirect cost allotment.

e. **Billing of Funding Agencies**

Responsibility for billing granting agencies for obligations owed the institution will rest initially with the institution's Finance Office. The Financial Office, if necessary, may refer accounts to the Director of Sponsored Programs who will be responsible, together with the project director, for requesting payment from the granting agency.

f. **Travel Expenditures on Grant Budgets**

1. A maximum of $35 per diem will be allowed on living expenses (accommodations and meals).

2. Direct cost of travel can be covered including air coach, rental cars, personal car at 12¢ per mile, taxis, and parking fees, where permitted by the granting agency.

5. **Grant and Contract Policy**

a. The Director of Sponsored Programs has primary responsibility for interpreting and administering policies and procedures in connection with financial management of grant projects.

b. Review and approval of project budgets and verifications of all expenditures under these budgets is the responsibility of the Office of Sponsored Programs. The project director, however, is also responsible for checking the most recent expenditure report before submitting a request for payment, so that all expenditures conform and are within the limits of the budget.

c. The Financial Vice-President is responsible for administration of overall institution financial management policies. In the case of possible conflict between grant management policy and overall institution policy, the Financial Vice-President and Director of Sponsored Programs would cooperate to resolve any conflict. Any issues remaining unresolved will be referred to the Executive Vice-President. In no case, however, may grant funds be disbursed without the written approval of the project director.

d. The Board of Directors regularly reviews the guidelines, procedures, and policies for sponsored grants and contracts. When changes have been approved, according to procedures outlined, they will be announced in Research Reports issued monthly by the Office of Sponsored Programs and will take effect at that time.

About the Publisher

Public Service Materials Center was established in 1967 to meet a need for useful and informative materials relating to fund raising development. In addition to "How to Get Government Grants," publications currently available from PSMC include the following:

WHERE AMERICA'S LARGE FOUNDATIONS
MAKE THEIR GRANTS (1974-75 Edition)

This is the most complete representative record ever published giving the specifics of grant-making by leading foundations in this country. It includes over 750 foundations in every part of the nation with assets of $1 million or more. $14.75

THE NEW HOW TO RAISE FUNDS FROM
FOUNDATIONS by Joseph Dermer

Written in practical, down-to-earth language, this manual covers all aspects of foundation fund raising from getting appointments to writing proposals. It is now recognized as a classic in its field. $8.95

HOW TO WRITE SUCCESSFUL FOUNDATION PRESENTATIONS by Joseph Dermer

Here are step-by-step instructions in writing successful foundation presentations, together with full examples of grant-winning proposals. Subjects covered include writing appointment letters, presentations for general operating funds, special projects, capital funds, as well as others. $8.95

THE 1972-73 SURVEY OF GRANT-MAKING FOUNDATIONS

The 1972-73 Survey of Grant-Making Foundations, compiled by Public Service Materials Center, contains vital information nowhere else available. Listed are over 1,000 foundations with such information as the best time of year to approach them, whether they make general operating grants, whether they will give you an appointment, and to whom you should write. $7.95

HOW TO GET YOUR FAIR SHARE OF FOUNDATION GRANTS by nine top experts

Never before has such an array of foundation experts appeared in one book. The purpose: to tell you — in simple, precise language — how to secure foundation grants. For this is no random collection of articles. Rather, each expert wrote on an assigned subject — to form part of a whole. The book begins with a full examination of the current foundation scene — and then moves step by step through the process you should use to obtain a grant. $12.00

THE COMPLETE FUND RAISING GUIDE
by Howard R. Mirkin
Drawing on a rich, varied background, one of America's leading fund raisers spells out the specifics of conducting virtually every kind of fund raising campaign including raising funds from government, business and labor, foundations and the general public. $12.50

NOTES

NOTES

NOTES